Optimizing Leadership Competency in Public Organizations

Concepts, Strategies, and Ethics

Chima Imoh, PhD. (Public Policy and Leadership)

Heritage Publishing Company

Houston, United States of America

Heritage Publishing Company,
7447 Harwin Drive,
Houston, TX 77036.

Library of Congress Control Number: 20169011323

Imoh, Chima

Optimizing Leadership Competency in Public Organizations/Chima Imoh

P.cm.-(Power, leadership, public organizations, and ethics)

ISBN-978-09854792-5-1

1. Leadership-public organizations-strategies-ethics.
2. Power in organizations-complex adaptive systens-motivation-decision making. I. Title. II. Series

Printed in the United States of America

PREFACE

The quests for the appropriate styles of leadership have always constituted major challenges to public organizations; as well as to public officials in the discharge of their public duties. Leadership skills are the abilities to identify the various concerns of followers or subordinates; and the knack of seeking the opportunities embedded in every problem. Obviously, public leaders in both the political and organizational arenas should always be concerned with issues that have meaning to people and endeavor to carry the people along. The perspectives of leadership styles that serve the interests of an organization or society have, however, always been subjects of debates. Most of the arguments focus on the authenticity and the transformativeness of any leadership style; as well as the appropriate organizational structures and behaviors to nurture and sustain each leadership style.

The natures and forms of organizations, however, have some bearing to their internal dynamics, especially leadership. The classifications of organizations, therefore, bear some relevance to the kind of leadership that would thrive within. The contemporary concepts of these organizational structures and behaviors include the recruitment and retention structures; the delegation of authority from the leadership to line managers; the effective motivational and reward systems; and the encouragement of employee participation in decision making.

The leaderships of public organizations are the implementers of public policies; hence their motivation and job satisfaction do affect the efficiency and quality of the services they offer to the citizenry. The leadership styles in public organizations, in turn, do affect the levels of motivation and empowerment derivable by the employees and subordinates. This being the case, the processes of creating strategic leadership and managing organizational changes require employee motivation. Moreso, motivational empowerment, which entails the involvement of members of staff at every level in the decision-making, allows organization to tap into the creativity and energy of the employees.

Often, organizational strategies have failed because of the lack of the appropriate leadership and employee involvement. Effective public leadership must address the needs and aspirations of the employees, followers, or the public as leadership is inseparable from their needs and goals. Everybody would have more say, and hence, contribute more to the organizational goals, thereby increasing organizational performance. This empowers the employees; and by so doing, the total effective power of the organization increases.

Public organizations need to develop the strategies that create the enabling environment for high involvement leadership through employee empowerment. This in turn, creates more positive feeling about work and the organization; more job satisfaction; and greater commitment to the organization. This also improves employee motivation and leadership-followership authenticity.

There has been much effort at understanding organizational changes with regard to its phases and the roles of leadership; and for this, numerous change management strategies have been developed namely; building blocks strategy, culture of excellence strategy, top-down strategy, power equalization strategy, and complex adaptive strategy. The focus of engineering the strategic changes in public organizations should always be on serving the nation and its citizens better.

In today's political and administrative environment, it is becoming more difficult to be as effective as required without acquiring the readiness for the continual changes that occur in the internal and external environments of modern societies. The purposes of managing changes have always been to preserve the organization, improve its cost leadership on its services, and maintain its core competencies.

The key to success in managing organizational changes is a motivated and highly trained workforce, and a leadership that aligns with tried and tested management principles and practices. A way forward is always to identify the employees' needs, fears and potentials; and to allay those fears and harness the potentials. Another necessity is the employment of modern day technological processes that are needed for managing and sustaining any changes. When all the necessary ingredients of change and the right leadership are available, creating the right balance and synergies among organizational processes always assures success.

Essentially, leaderships in public organizations should be viewed as processes rather than positions. As such, organizational leaderships need to involve employees in the decision-making processes, giving everybody more opportunities to contribute to the organizational goals. Usually, the strategies to actualize this would include the creation and implementation of communication strategies that consistently communicate the visions and strategic plans to employees.

The purpose of the book is to discuss the strategies for optimizing leadership competences in public organizations; as well the abilities and roles of leaderships in enabling the effective mangement and propulsion of the organization toward positive changes. This book explores various leadership theories and competences; and how they affect and enable the engineering and management of changes in organizations. There are extensive discussions on the effects of leadership on the ability of the public organizations to 'strategize' and manage organizational changes. The book also analyzes the theory and classification of organizations, theories of motivation, theories of change management; and the theories of power, ethics, and culture; as they relate to the optimization of leadership competences in public organizations.

There are various theories to explore these changes; as well as their relationships to organizational leaderships and employees' motivation. This book also engages in concise discourses to show that, sometimes, the combinations of leadership competences are required for particular environments and circumstances.

Although there is a measure of acceptance on the advantages of various leadership styles over others, efforts have been made in this book to address the challenges that respectively confront each of them. Subsequently, there are effective leadership competences to adopt for optimizing leadership; as well as creating and managing organizational changes. Obviously, the effectiveness of leadership in fostering changes depends on such values as transparency, honesty, altruism, accessibility, followers' perceptions and level of ethics. To optimize the effectiveness of their actions, these values are those leaders need to bring to bear on public organizations. Generally, effective and sound leadership performances are better enhanced under the auspices of ethical organizations.

Chima Imoh, PhD.

ABOUT THE AUTHOR

Dr Chima Imoh has a degree in Geodetic Engineering and a master's degree in international management. He has a doctorate degree in Public policy and Administration, specializing in public management and leadership. Dr Imoh is a member of the National Honor Society for Public Affairs and Administration, United States of America.

He has lectured and worked in public institutions in the United States and in Africa. His practice expertise is on public policies for national development; a specialized field in which he consults for organizations and public think tanks that work on national development policies; especially for developing countries.

Dr Chima Imoh is the author of other four books: (i) *Cultural Competence for Global Management, (ii) Policymaking and Development Strategies for Local Governments in Nigeria, (iii) Elections, Leadership, and National development in Nigeria, and (iv) Nigeria: Politics and Policies for National Development*. He is also a co-author of the book, *Competency for Public Administration,* edited by Professors Susan T. Gooden and Kris Major.

CONTENTS

PART III:
Leadership Models for Public Organizations and Public Services

PART IV: Power and Politics in Public Organizations

PART I:

MODERN PUBLIC ORGANIZATIONS:

Forms, Change Management, and Motivation

Chapter 1

Concepts, Forms and Nature of Public Organizations

Organizational theories are used to understand organizations; and the nature of the changes that occur within them and their environments. Modern day bureaucracies are essentially based on the classical organization theory- the first theory of organizational management[8]. Bureaucracies, individually or collectively refer to the totality of government offices, including the individual organizations; or to all government officials both elected or appointed[8]. Modern bureaucracies have their roots in Europe when the governing of the Kingdoms became so complicated that it became necessary for the Kings to delegate authorities to their representatives[8]. From all indications, most bureaucracies in the world today have recovered from this non-democratic origin. A fully developed bureaucracy can essentially be described as a form of organization with specific set of structural arrangements[8].

All organizations, both private and public, are formal structures in so far as they represent 'rationally ordered instruments for the achievement of stated goals'[6]. Consequently, organizations can be described as the arrangement of material and personnel resources for accomplishing stated purposes through the allocation of functions and responsibilities[6]. A public organization can thus, be viewed as the arrangement of human and material resources for the attainment of stated purposes through the allocation of resources, functions, and responsibilities in furtherance of public and common good. All public organizations should, however, be guided by the principles of management that reflect the national values and the cultural environment of their performance systems[8].

Structural Classifications

To have a better grasp of such public management concepts as; dissolution of power, employee empowerment, and employee motivation; an understanding of the structural classifications of the organization would be necessary. The forms of public organizations can be viewed and organized from such three perspectives as: a rigid structure, an adaptive social structure, or as an economy. The structural organization theory views the organization as a rational structure; the systems theory views the organization as an adaptive social system; and the organization economics theory views the organization as an economy. Under their regulatory functions, it is also necessary for leaders in some public organizations to understand the classifications of private entities from ethical standpoints.

Structural Organization Theory

The structural organization theory sees the organizations as rational institutions whose primary purposes are to accomplish definite objectives[8]. The structural organization theory is more concerned with the vertical and horizontal differentiation of the organization. The vertical differentiation deals with such issues as the hierarchical levels of authority and coordination. Horizontal differentiation deals with differences between organizational units; especially with regards to product/service lines, geographical locations, or skills.This structural organization approach proposes that rational organizational behavior is best achieved through systems of defined rules and formal authority[8]. Under this theory, organizational control and coordination are very essential for the maintenance of organizational rationality[8].

The theory also proposes that specialization and division of labor are essential as they increase the quality and quantity of services or operations. As the theory projects, the most appropriate structure is dependent on its given objectives and is environmental conditions. Moreover, when the existing systems have structural flaws; changing the organizational structure becomes the reasonable solution.

The organizational perspectives of mechanistic and organic systems were developed from this theory of structural organization. Mechanistic organizations are rigid bureaucracies that operate on strict rules, with tasks defined in very narrow manners; and where the system of communication is from top to down[4]. Organic organizations on the other hand, encourage flexible work flows and broad definition of tasks[4].

The adoption of the mechanistic form of organization is most appropriate where the conditions are stable and there is the possibility of using patterns of heirarchy; with reliance on formal rules and regulations, and structured decision-making processes[8]. On the other hand, the adoption of the organic form of organization is more appropriate where the conditions are more dynamic; such as rapidly changing environments, creating the necessity for less rigidity, more participation; in which workers can define and redefine their positions and relationships[8]. Although most public organizations in the United States operate as mechanistic systems; such organizations as the Federal Emergency Management Agency (F.E.M.A.) and the National Counterterrorism Center (NCTC) would require the organic approach.

Systems theory

The system theory perceives an organization as complex sets of interconnected elements; with interlocking inputs, processes, outputs, and the operational environment being in continuous and ever-changing interactions[7]. The system theory seeks to understand the relationship among organizations; as well as the prevailing internal and environmental variables. The system theory also focuses on the underlying processes within and between organizations[7].

The system theories tend to be complex and multi-dimensional in their assumptions of the cause-effects dynamics within an organization[8]. Since, organizations are not static but are rather in constantly shifting states of dynamic equilibrium, a change in one of the interacting elements tends to trigger off changes in the other elements[7]. Even fluctautions from outside will force the system to adjust to maintain equilibrium[2]. From this perspective, the processes within a system are so interrelated and interconnected that decisions made to alter one part would affect the other parts as well[5].

In a public organization, the nature of the change can be as strategic as the offering new service lines; as tactical as developing closer relationships with the citizens; or as such cultural adjustments as initiating motivation programs for employees[2]. Under this system, when management makes decisions involving one organizational element, unanticipated impacts could occur throughout the systems of the organization[8]. This could even create more unforseen impacts. System theorists analyze these interconnections and potential unanticipated impacts, using the information and decision making processes of the organization as their focal points[7].

From its organizational element, the system theory essentially views an organization from the perspective of ever-changing interconnected elements in an operational environment in a state of dynamic equilibrium; and disrupting this equilibrium (through changes in one of the elements) would trigger other foreseen or unforeseen changes. Under this organizational element, the system theory is basicallly concerned with the issues of relationships and interdependence of the processes and structures.

From its human elements, they are the organizational behaviors that examine how people act, their motivation, and interactions with others. It hence provides the basic tools, skills, ideas, and strategies for assessing and managing human behavior in organizations[1]. As these constitute the human elements of the system theory, a change in organizational behavior will trigger off changes in the other inputs of the system; and would ultimately affect the output.

In applying this to public organizations, the main component of the system theory is the emphasis on using quantitative tools to understand the relationship among public organizations and the prevailing environmental variables with regards to inputs and outputs[7]. Such inputs would include human and financial resources, information flows or technology; and such outputs as products, services, regulations, edicts, and laws. Depending on the prevailing environment, the outputs from the public organizations have varying impacts on the citizens, political leaders, families, business, other public organizations, and the society in general. Sometimes, such outputs as immigration laws even affect the citizens of other nations.

When applied to public organizations, system theory essentially posits that immediate societal problems are usually dependent on the environment; and are also affected by some other components of the social system. Viewed from the side of social systems, the system theory does share common grounds with the procedural perspective to social change management, which focuses on the relationship between the individuals, groups, and the society.

The system theory is also useful for assessing the need for organizational change because it can guide change agents in considering how a change in one part of the organization would impart on the other aspects[7]. To remain responsive to the needs and demands of the citizens, public organizations will always need to undergo constant improvement processes. An understanding of the system theory would guide the public administrator in the appreciation of the effect a change in one input would have on the other inputs; as well as on the outputs. Of course, this would equally give the administrator an insight into the effect of the outputs on the society at large.

The application of the concept of system theories into public organizations could, however, introduce power play and politics into the social change processes; and can lead to conflicts. The system theory does not, however, condemn conflicts and political struggles; but rather regard them as a bulwark against stagnation. Conflicts are essential for growth and change; and are the primary defense a system has against stagnation, entropy, and eventual extinction[1]. The system theory perceives conflicts as aspects of the larger system of interactions in which conflicts and adaptation are inseparable. Public organizations should, to an extent, be re-oriented as adaptive systems that are part of their environment; and they must adapt to their environments if they are to remain relevant to the purposes of their legislations and public services.

Organizational economics theory

In the consideration of an organization as an economy, it can be viewed as a system of relationships that define the availability of scarce resources; and which can be manipulated in terms of efficiency and effectiveness[7]. Essentially, organizational economics theory seeks to explain the behavior of an organization, and the behavior within an organization. The organizational economics theory also views organization from the perspective of any events or processes that exhibit regular patterns and structures[7]. From this perspective, examining public organizations would include the activities within the organizations; as well as between the organization and the other public or government bureaucracies[7]. In general terms, organization economics theory also deals with how to motivate employees to act in the best interest of the owners (in private organizations) or the public (in public organizations). The core elements and underlying theories that define organizational economics are; the agency theory, the theory of property rights, and the transaction cost theory[7].

The agency theory posits that the managers and employees are agents of owners. The owners, as a matter of neccessity, must delegate some authority to the agents who are expected to act in the best interest of the owners. For public organizations, the assumption is that the agents (public administrators) will always act in the interest of the owners (public). Sometimes, however, these agents do not act in the best interest of the public. Consequently, the agency theory advocates the use of such mechanisms as incentives and monitoring to motivate as well as 'limit the aberrant activities of the agents'[7].

Property rights constitute another core element of the organizational economics theory. As a public organization is a legal entity with complex and multiple relationships with owners of labor, material, capital, and intellectual inputs; the rights to property become core elements of the organizational economics theory. The theory of property rights also deals with the allocation of costs and rewards within organizations.

The transaction cost theory deals with how to maintain the owner-agent relationship and minimize costs; and their effects on management decision-making processes[7]. Since an organization can be cheated either through contracts or the activities of agents, other mechnisms must be used to minimize costs[7]. These mechanisms may include pre-contract, post-contracts, and ethical safeguards. The range of considerations in the organizational economics theory is obviously larger than the range of the system theory as its transaction dimensions are not limited.

Ethical Classifications

For the purposes of developing and enforcing public policies, it is necessary for the public administrator to understand the ethical classification of organizations as it applies to both private and public entities. Organizations can also be classified from the perspectives of their ethical progress as; immoral, amoral, legalistic, responsive, emergent ethical, and ethical. The immoral organizations are those whose approaches tend to create the impression of a positive and active opposition to what is ethical. Their motives are selfish and their goals are "success at all costs". Such organizations consider ethical regulations as constituting constraints and barriers to business; and exploit every opportunity to circumvent such ethical regulations. A typical example of this kind of organization was the defunct Houston-based Enron. The leadership of Enron Corporation was falsifying its financial books in regards to its profitability, debt; and its use of Special Purpose Entities (SPEs) - the off-book partnerships used to hide debts and losses.

The amoral organizations largely ignore ethical concerns; focusing solely on productivity and profit[3]. The policies of the leaderships of such organizations are neither distinctively moral nor immoral; with decisions lying outside the moral order of particular codes of conduct. To such organizations, fines, and penalties are not ethical indictments; but rather the cost of doing business. The policies of such organizations are usually selfish. Even if their motives are well intentioned; the policies of such organizations are usually self-serving.

The legalistic organizations tend to equate ethics with following the rules and regulations, while protecting their organizations[3]. Such organizations tend to act as that, "there is no morality in business, only legality". Examples of such organizations are those gun-manufacturing companies that do not consider it an ethical issue to add more personalized safety measures (like thump print activators) on their guns. Others are the tobaco companies and large grocery chains who believe that there is nothing wrong with manufacturing or selling cigarretes so long as it is not prohibited by the law.

Responsive organizations are usually concerned with the perception of positive corporate social responsibility, rather than being proactively responsible. They focus on been seen as socially responsible in reacting to public issues and problems; but do not develop ethical platforms nor make proactive efforts to foster ethical environments.

The emergent ethical organizations are those that make proactive efforts to create ethical environments. These organizations institute various ethical platforms to ensure ethical behaviors. They use ombudspersons, code of ethics, or ethical value handbooks to emphasize and enforce ethics. Such companies as Johnson and Johnson have established codes of ethics.

The ethical organizations exhibit the highest level of moral development. Such organizations incorporate ethical cultures in all the processes and actions. They make conscious efforts to succeed by operating, not only within the confines of the law; but also with the sound ethical precepts of fairness and justice. They operate within the confines of the due processes of both the law and morality.

Chapter 2

Public Organizations as Complex Adaptive Systems

The concept of complex adaptive system (CAS) is a modern adaptation and expansion of the system theory. A CAS is a large collection of diverse parts, interconnected in such a hierarchical manner that the organization grows over time without a centralized control[5]. The concept hinges on the premise that the operations of systems are expected to be at the edge of chaos; changing continuously, and adapting to the external environment. As organizations are "living organisms" in the social and institutional complex systems to which they relate; their boundaries are therefore, permeable; permitting energy, information and other inputs/outputs to enter and leave through multiple channels. A CAS can, therefore, be used to understand organizations and the nature of their changes.

The Concepts of Complex Adaptive Systems

Usually, when the internal and external environments of an organization are stable, the organization becomes less responsive to changes[8]. So, by evoking higher levels of experimentation and mutation, and moving toward the edge of choas, the components of the organization self-organize, giving rise to new forms[8]. Although, the outcomes of these experimentations and mutations may not necessarily be along a linear path, they can rather be disturbed in a manner that tends toward the desired outcomes[8]. The field of complex adaptive systems theory seeks to understand how order emerges from these non-linear complex living systems even when they operate at the edge of chaos. With the changes in technology being so swift and continuous, organizations have to operate at the "edge of chaos" to respond to the changes[10].

The system is complex; as its structures go through processes of change that cannot be described by a single rule, and its emerging features cannot be predicted from the current description of the structures[2]. Complex systems are usually self-organizing, non-linear, and exhibit order/chaos dynamics, as well as being emergent. Often, such systems involve large numbers of elements that are engaged in structures that can also exist on many scales. All the elements interact locally, and are connected; even though such connections may be indirect. As an adaptive system, it changes in the face of changes in the environment; so as to maintain some kind of survival by altering its properties and modifying its environment[2]. In a CAS, the units or elements interact, adapt, and undergo natural selection in response to the environment. A complex system could be a government or its entities, an economy, family, or the human system.

Essentially, the CAS is a collection of elements or units acting interconnectively in a variety of predictable and unpredictable ways. The examples of CAS include: families, colleges, workplaces, churches, unions, stock market, private and public organizations, and political parties. Other examples include social systems, cultures, technologies, traffic, and weather. The elements and individuals in these systems; such as relatives, professors, stock traders, church-goers, workers, or political parties work together to create interdependent behaviours that lead to self-organization. We may probably have to imagine the edge of chaos and crisis of centuries of slavery, degradation, discrimination and segregation against Blacks (African-Americans) in the United States; which suddenly emerged into the order of the civil rights proclamation of the 1960s.

Nature and Form of Complex adaptive systems

The complex adaptive system theory gives a considerable insight into how human systems may organize themselves to respond and adapt to external changes[12]. The capabilities of a system and its components to adjust and become fitted for responses to the environment also constitute part of the system. Understanding the CAS is a viable method for modeling complex organizations toward understanding their behaviours; based on observed information and data. The CAS therefore, enables the analytical evaluation of the organization system from a more holistic perspective[3].

The CAS is also a concept of building the capacity for mindfulness in the organizations; and which can be analyzed from the perspective of the four complex adaptive system principles, namely; dynamic instability, emphasis on the whole, self-organization, and continuous energy transformation[12]. These capacities, which are shaped by, and also adopt to the external environments; include skills, systems, processes,relationships, values, norms, ambitions, power, and leadership.

The dynamic instability sees the organization as being unstable and in a continous state of adaptation and evolution with regard to its environment. The complex adaptive principle of laying emphasis on the whole indicates that small changes will interact with each other in the external environment, growing in intensity until the system reaches the critical decision points at which an entity has the option of choosing a new direction from several alternatives[12]. The complexity results from the inter-relationship, interactions, and inter-connectivity of the elements within the system; and between the system and its environment[2]. A decision or action by one part within the system will influence all other related parts even though it may not be in any uniform pattern[2].

Self-organization is a process by which a structure or pattern emerges in an open system without specifications from the outside environment[5]. Self-organization can also be described as a natural way by which CAS progresses from its choatic and disorganized state to an organized and differentiated state[5]. The system maintains its essential identity as it undergoes the self-induced non-linear transformation[5]. The self-organization principle also describes a situation, in which there is no planning or managing; but rather constantly re-organizing as to find the best fit with the environment. In keeping with the complexity theory of change management, it is noteworthy that even when there is this constant chaos, creating the appropriate order-generating rules permits the needed self-organization that allows the system to succeed. The self-organizing principle of CAS is always influenced by positive feedbacks that are self re-inforcing. Let it be noted, however, that a successful self-organization for the entire systen can produce undesirable outcomes for its individual units or for the other related CAS[4]. Leadership is crucial to the process of self-organization as leaders may serve as the designers of the learning experiences[10].

Finally, continous energy transformation occurs when the organization discards its old ways; and embraces the new ways and new values. An organization operating on the principles of complex adaptive system can continue to develop with its environment so long as it can remain open to new energy from its environment[12]. Under a complex adaptive system, responsiveness to the environment is the measure of value[6].

Public organizations as Learning Organizations

A CAS is essentially composed of interacting elements following rules, but exchanging influence with other local elements and the environment; and altering the immediate influence that they are responding to; by virtue of their simple actions[10]. The need to design and apply complex adaptive systems on the processes of modern public organizations will always exist. To create a better understanding of the CAS concept, however, it would be necessary to first analyze the theory of appreciative inquiry, which is the core process of an adaptive organization.

The theory of appreciative inquiry pre-supposes a collaborative and participative approach to seeking, identifying, and elevating the supportive forces that are present when a system is performing at optimal levels in terms of organizational goals[9]. The essence of appreciative inquiry is to facilitate organizational change by encouraging the stakeholders of an organization to explore the positive capacities within the organization[9]. The strenght of appreciative inquiry lies in creating change; with the primary focus on the assets of the organization.

To become a learning organization, there is need to create an appreciative inquiry process; a tool that helps learning organizations engage in the processes and dialogues that possess the likelihood of uncovering the forces of positive change. Such organizations would have to adopt the, "learning perspective" of appreciative inquiry. Ultimately, appreciative inquiry provides the intellectual platform that gives organizations an expanded way of viewing reality and the rationale; and a method for creating the desired future[13].

The wide spread use of technology has warranted the designation of public organizations as complex adaptive systems. Through the dynamic and continous processes, the individual elements or units within the system garner information from other units or from the external environment. These pieces of information are subjected to internal rules; and responses are formulated to generate properties that are used to strenghten the system; while eliminating the properties that are not needed. In this manner, the CAS creates potential changes and adaptation through the alteration of its rules or through the modification of the external environment.

Being a CAS entails that new inputs in the processes of a public organization; such as those occassioned by policy changes, will always result to both predictable and unpredictable outcomes. The focus is for leaders to watch out for the positive outcomes and use them to reinforce the processes; while discarding the negative outcomes.

In public organizations, the changing (second) stage of Lewin's theory is essentially about introducing and helping public service implementers to learn the new techniques, behaviors, attitudes, and processes. These public organizations can, therefore, be made to become learning organization. Becoming learning organizations entail the creation of appreciative inquiry processes that would, in turn, enable them engage in meaningful dialogue to uncover forces of positive change. Creating a learning organization also requires effective feedback mechanisms. The feedback mechanism should include the outcomes from "integrative resistance" whereby the information obtained from the employees' resistance to change is used to design improvements to the processes. This stage could sometimes involve the benchmarking of organizational performances against the performance of the best public organizations in the bureaucracy. Unfortunately, most public organizations are locked in rigid order; and as such not easily capable of evolution.

The learning process for market-oriented public organizations such as the United States Postal Services (USPS) will involve the understanding its environments. This includes not only the macro environment; but also the analysis of the industry and competitor, analysis of the consumer and consumer pattern, product inventions, and the analysis of the internal environment. This entails the collation of the relevant data and analysis of such data as they affect the industry; which usually provides the tactical and strategic intelligence needed for the determination of organizational strategy. The benefit of this activity includes fostering and understanding the effects of change in the organization; assisting forecasting, and bringing expectation of change to bear on decision-making.

The complex adaptive organization requires the holistic understanding of the organization in relationship to its environment[12]. An affective environmental scanning program would enable the decision maker to understand current and potential changes taking place in their external environments[6]. From this perspective, an effective organizational leader also has to be an effective learner. The design, structuring, and implementation of leadership development programs should always take this into cognizance. There should be a strong relationship between learning and leadership; as leadership is an ongoing learning process[1]. Considering that public organizations derive existence and responsibilities from legislative actions and therefore bear some restraining checks and balances, it would be daunting, but not impossible a task for most public organizations to adopt the complex adaptive system model for change management.

Essentially, any public organization that embraces the structures of an adaptive system adjusts through its own self-organizing characteristics that usually come from the inter-dependency of its sub-systems[10]. Whereas the traditional organizational structures are designed to control behaviours, complex adaptive systems are in themselves, constituted by changeable structures. Leaders of public organizations must, therefore, refocus these organizations from the old hierarchical systems to dynamic systems in which leaders can change the structure, culture, and strategies to meet the dynamic environments in which they now operate[4]. Taking a public organization from the hierarchical structure to a dynamic structure, however, requires the appreciation and acknowlededgement that the old system has been unable to produce the best desirable outcomes.

Chapter 3

Theories of Organizational Change

Change management is the process of continually renewing, not only the direction and structure of an organization; but also its capacities to serve the ever-changing needs of its environment, employees, or stakeholders[14]. Change management usually comes about because an organization needs to make a change from one type of culture to another, or it needs to incorporate another culture type[6]. These changes would entail the creation of new behaviors, new working methods, and new performance levels that would persist for a period that suits the setting[3]. These changes, however, always do create resistance from employees and other stakeholders. For the change process to be successful, these resistances will have to be overcome.

Perspectives to Change Management

Some theories and perepectives to change management include Lewin's change theories, culture-excellence approach, the processual approach, the complexity theories, the evolutionary theory, and the episodic/continous theories.

Lewin's change management theory

The Lewin's theory of change management rests on a three-model structure of unfreezing, changing, and freezing. The 'unfreezing' stage focuses on creating the motivation for change and in so doing; encouraging individuals to replace old behaviors and attitudes with those desired by management[11]. The changing stage is essentially about introducing and helping employees to learn the new techniques, behaviors, attitudes, and processes. The last stage, the freezing stage, involves stabilizing the changes and giving the employees a chance to exhibit and practice the new attitudes and behaviors. When undergoing changes, the key to resolving conflicts is to facilitate planned change through learning, so as to enable the individuals understand the new perspectives; thereby restructuring their perceptions[4].

Culture-Excellence Approach

This perspective, developed by Robert Waterman, tends to equate organizational success with the possession of a strong and appropriate organizational culture[5]. This is a newer perspective to change management. The proponents argue that organizations lose their competitive edges when they become too bureaucratic, inflexible, unresponsive, or slow to change. They go further to argue that organizations need to configure themselves to build internal and external synergies; which encourage a spirit of innovation, experimentation, and entrepreneurship by creating the appropriate organizational culture[15]. These proponents of the culture-excellence approach propose that the command-and-control style of management be discouraged. In its stead, they argue that organizational objectives be promoted by loose controls, based on shared values and culture; and pursued through employee empowerment[16].

The Processual Approach

This is a perspective to change management, which, focuses on the relationship between the individuals, groups, and the society[7]. The proponents particularly claim that organizational changes are complex processes that involve decision-making, individual perceptions, political struggles, coalition and collaboration; and thus likely to be procedural[10].

The evolutionary theory

Some social scientists have argued for the evolutionary perspective to organizational change. This perspective views changes as transitional, transformational, or developmental. Like the procedural theorist, transitional changes represent small, gradual, and incremental changes in policies, people, procedures, or structures[9]. On the other hand, transformational changes involve radical shifts in underlying assumptions, deep-rooted mindsets, cultures, or other organizational behaviors[12]. Developmental changes flow from a philosophy of nugging leaders toward a culture of continuous, dynamic and yet manageable changes that are most likely to create continuous growth and development[1].

Episodic/Continuous Theories

Some other scientists, however, indicate that organizational changes could be either episodic or continuous[17]. Although, radical episodic changes are not always frequent, they usually have greater intensity[13]. In contrast, continuous changes, although incremental, are unending. The adverse environmental issues that constitute threats to organizational survival would demand episodic changes; whereas more common events may demand the less intense continuous change response[13].

The complexity Theories

The complexity theories as they affect organizational changes are hinged on the postulation that nature is constantly in chaos and in order-disorder sequences. The need arises to create order-generating rules that usher in some measure of managed order. When, therefore, a complex system operates at the edge of chaos, creativity and growth attain their optimum levels[8]. Obviously, when there is this constant chaos, these order-generating rules, if appropriate, permit self-organization to take place; allowing the system to succeed, whereas others fall over the edge[4]. The organizations that relentlessly pursue a path of continuous innovation succeed because, by operating at the edge of chaos, they inject much novelty and change into their normal operations[8]. The complexity theories are quite widely practiced and are, increasingly being used as a way of understanding and changing organizations[2].

Chapter 4

Models for Implementing Changes in Public Organizations

Organizations are constantly in need of changes; hence the ability to manage these changes has become a core competence for successful organizations. Startling breakthroughs in information technology are forcing both private and public organizations to change the way they do business or provide essential services[4]. Change management in organizations call for changes in the cultures of the organizations; including the patterns of enduring believes, norms, values, and assumptions; both formal and informal, which the organizations have adopted[1]. Most times, sweeping changes are needed when an organization needs to make a change from one set of values and behaviours to another. A way to determine if changes are needed is to monitor continuously, such drivers of change as the introduction of new technological processes, changes in operating environments, failures in meeting objectives, or deviations from the appropriate organizational culture.

The basic goal of change process is to make fundamental changes on how organizations operate to cope with new and challenging environments[3]. John Kotter had developed an eight-step model for leading organizational changes[3]. The model postulates that change processes go through phases that require some considerable measure of time. Although the Kotter's change mode is more specific, it could be taken as a more detailed format of the Lewin's model of change[4].

Organizational Change Models
The strategies for creating and managing organizational changes come from different perspectives. The underlying essence of these perspectives are all indicative of the fact that organizations lose their abilities to perform optimally when they become too bureaucratic,

inflexible, or slow to change. The stategic approaches for implementing changes in public organizations would include; building blocks strategy, culture of excellence, top-down, power equalization, and complex adaptive strategies. The evaluation of the ability of public organizations to enable change by adopting any of these strategies is important from both the perspective of facilitation and that of accountability[5].

Building Blocks strategy

Kurt Lewin's strategy of "building blocks for strategic change", which entails creating new and piece-by-piece view of the organizational vision is quite appropriate for most public organizations. The concept envisions strategic changes that stem from increments of action, through the provocation of pressure points, or through offers of better opportunities[2]. Essentially, the stimulus for change emanates from the presence of a series of building blocks that constitute the forces of change[2]. Transformation occurs in three sequential steps of unfreezing and aligning; discovering and sharing; and committing and tracking. The three stages create the motivation for change: introducing and helping employees to learn the new techniques; stabilizing the changes; and giving the employees a chance to exhibit and practice the new attitudes and behaviors. The continuous change concepts of this change strategy are suitable to the nature and public functions of public organizations.

Culture of Excellence Strategy

As a strategy, the newer excellence culture perspective suggests that public organizations lose their effectiveness when they become too bureaucratic. In order to flourish even when others falter, a strategically-led public organization must adjust its bureaucracies and strategies to defeat criss and conquer environmental turbulences[2]. Proponents of this stratregy have argued that public organizations need to configure toward responsiveness and innovation by creating the appropriate organizational culture. This strategy, however, is more appropriate for the market-oriented public organizations.

The Top-down Strategy

The top-down strategy of change management characterizes the unilateral use of power. Change implementations are carried out through the authority derived from hierarchical positions. The upper echelons of leadership identify problems and proffer solutions; and then direct such solutions downward through formal control mechanisms. The top-down change implementation strategies work best when the change must be accomplished more quickly, when the need for change is organization-wide, and the knowledge of the process is concentrated at the top or the change agent has an enormous power base[6].

The power Equalization Strategy

Power equalizations strategies come from two perspectives: shared power, in which authority is vested at the top management; and delegated power, in which authority is delegated. Shared power involves some interactions and power-sharing between top management and the subordinates. In the delegated power model, almost complete authority and responsibility for identifying and acting on problems are delegated to subordinates. The positive outcome of delegation of power model is employee empowerment. This form of change implementation is more successful when no time pressure exists, when the need for change is not organization wide, when the knowledge to implement changes is widely dispersed, or the change agent has small power base[6].

The Complex Adaptive Strategy

The complex adaptive strategy as it affects change management in public organizations anchors on the assumption that nature is constantly in chaos and in order-disorder sequences. The strategic responsibility of the leadership of public organizations is to remain conscious and responsive to the ambient environment; to identify and understand the implications of change, to determine the courses of action; as well as guide their implementation[2]. This strategy conforms to complexity theory and complex adaptive system approach to change management; which are sometimes, considered unsuitable for public organizations for reasons of their stability-oriented natures.

Chapter 5

Success Factors for Managing Change in Public Organizations

There could be potential resistances to any far-reaching changes in a public organization. Organizational changes create uncertainty with regard to the expected and acceptable behavioral tendencies of individuals[7]. Changes that modify existing authority, structures, role, and duties not only generate some measure of concern, but can also create ambiguity[10].

Other reasons employees may resist changes include fear of the unknown, self-interest, habit, selective attention and retention, and need for security[8]. On individual levels, employees are usually apprehensive of new structures and new ways of doing things. When innovative or radically different changes are introduced without warning, affected employees usually become fearful of the implications; and these fears usually create a great deal of résistance.

More so, sweeping changes to a job may intimidate an employee to the extent of creating doubts on his or her capability; and thus trigger-off a measure of resistance to such changes. Some employees would also be afraid of new and unknown yardsticks for performance measurements. Even when changes are not likely to affect some employees, such employees could still resist the changes if they are likely to affect their friends and co-workers. Cynical orientation about the motives and relevance of the change processes could also constitute a resistance to change.

On the organizational leadership level, threats to power and influence, lack of trust, resource limitations, different perceptions of goals and social disruptions are reasons why some organizational leaders resist changes. Sometimes, when administrative or technological changes are perceived to alter the bases and balances of power or threaten jobs, there are bound to be resistance to such changes, even at leadership levels. The leadership may unknowing create barriers to changes; especially, when the designed strategies undermine organizational values[5].

Changes can also make the leadership vulnerable if the changes entail actions that could disrupt their comfort zones within the organizations[5]. More often, the leader is both the enabler and victim of change[5]. For instance, changes that are adaptive are less threatening because they appear familiar; whereas unfamiliar innovative changes create anxieties[5]. Some organizational leaders can sometimes become resistant to change by becoming "paralyzed by the downside possibilities. They worry that employees with seniority will become defensive, that morale will drop, that events will spin out of control; and that they will be blamed for creating a crisis[4].

Although resistances to change are inevitable; with individuals expressing such resistances both covertly and overtly, some other key mistakes that impede change initiatives are complacency, lack of communication (both in words and actions), premature assumption of success, and distrust[1]. The resistance could be overcome if the organization has such capacities as effective leadership, enough change champions, internal support, and monitoring and control mechanism to drive it to the desired objectives. Essentially, when all the necessary ingredients of change are available, creating the right balance and synergies among organizational processes always assures success.

The Key Success Factors

The key success factors for managing change are the availability of change structures and change champions. Other success factors are effective communication strategies, motivating the employees to comit to the change process, job competence training, conflict resolution frameworks, and sustainability of the change process.

Availability of change Structures

Sometimes, leaders underestimate how hard it can be to drive people out of their comfort zones[4]. The required change structures include; clear responsibilities for change implementation and availability of strong improvement infrastructures. Essentially, there is the necessity to build up all the capabilities for meeting the new challenges.

Nominating Change Champions

A crucial and necessary consideration is whether or not the change processes have enough 'change champions' to lead it to the desired level. The appropriate strategy for achieving this is the nomination of high performing employees as change champions, empowered to act as process owners. The change process must be owned and led by those who have developed and possess the capacities to elevate the energy of the teams; as well as unleash the creativity of the individuals. These change champions will nurture, control, and monitor the change processes. The change champions will also identify and address the needs and concerns of the other employees. Generally, these change champions are more effective when they can guard against restricting the flow of information and ignoring other's ideas[6].

Effective communication Strategies

The leader would have to consider the attitude of the employees towards innovation and changes. Cynicism about the motives and relevance of the change processes can constitute a resistance to change. The strategies to manage these resistances would include the creation and implementation of communication strategies that consistently transmit the new vision and strategic plans to the employees. This can be achieved by creating organization-wide understanding of the need for change, as well as its positive implications.

Motivate Workforce toward Commitment to Change

No modern public organization can operate as effectively as required without having made itself ready for the continuous changes that prevail within it, as well as its external environments. The key to success in managing the changes is a motivated and highly trained workforce that is committed to the change management practices. Designing the processes to build the required commitment to change is an effective strategy. For an effective implementation of change, this can be done by motivating employees and providing effective communications on the on-going processsses[3c].

Employees' involvement

Involving the employees to the change management processes are of importance in meeting the organizational objectives. In trying to revamp the organizational strategies for change mangement, it is not enough to simply shift the staff around or root out inefficiencies[3a]. There is the more important imperative of preparing employees adequately for the change by involving them in the processes. Involving the employees in the change processes, which in turn, motivates them to make the transition to new attitudes and behaviors, is crucial to the success.

Job Competence Training

The fear of new job competency requirements can be overcome by offering competence training to the employees. Offering incentives for competency development and growth; such as offering variable pays based on competency can motivate the employees to improve their skills. Another necessity is the training of the employees in the use of the modern day technological processes that are needed for the change.

Leadership commitment and support

During an organizational change, the role of the leader is crucial and of immense importance. The importance of leadership manifests much more during the conception and management of the change projects, as well as during the management of innovations; especially in estabished public organizations[3d].

Clear and measurable objectives and responsibilities:

Having clear and measurable objectives is necessary for the smooth execution of the processes of change. It is therefore, necessary to articulate smart objectives to measure the degree of achievement. Moreover, setting objectives is a key step in the strategic planning and assessment of the change processes[3b]. It is also necessary to designate and define responsibilities. Otherwise, when employees do not know their roles and responsibilities, the workplace can become dysfunctional.

Well-designed Implementation plan

A well-designed implementation plan is a key to strategic success. Although, an effective strategy for implementation may be difficult, paying attention to plan execution across all levels of the organization is a worthy objective. This is more crucial as the leadership bears responsibility for successful or failed execution of the change processes.

Methods to evaluate, measure, and track results

There should also be methods to evaluate, measure, and track results of change programs. Observable variables such as productivity, efficiency, cost-effectiveness, and customer/citizen satisfaction may be used for the purposes of evaluating, measuring, and tracking the results of the change processes.

Conflicts Resolution Framework

There is need to have a framework for resolving any individual or unit conflicts that may arise during the change process. A key to resolving conflicts during organization changes are to facilitate the planned change through learning; thereby enabling the individuals to understand and re-orient their perceptions and behaviors to the goals and objectives of the organization[9].

Sustainability of change processes

The purpose of change is to preserve the organization; to improve its services to stakeholders and create value to the citizenry, as well as preserve its core competencies. If the needed change does not occur, everything might be lost. The change must be reconciled with continuity in order to preserve the entity[3]. This sustainability implies that "new working methods and performance levels persist for a period appropriate to the setting[2]. In analyzing organizational changes, it is worthy to note that the sustainability of positive changes implies that new behaviors, and new working procedures and performance levels created through leadership are maintained[2]. Whereas this sustainability may be beneficial, it could, however, become harmful to the organization whenever those methodologies and processes become obsolete.

Chapter 6

Strategies and Models for Workforce Motivation

Motivation can be described as those psychological processes that persistently cause voluntary actions that are directed to particular goals. Motivation usually culminates in the desire and intention of the individual to behave in particular ways[8]. Motivation is also that internal state that causes an individual to behave in a particular way to accomplish particular purposes and goals[5]. The motivation theories seek to explain the processes through which organizational goals are pursued and achieved[5].

The pioneers of workplace psychology, namely; Abraham Maslow, Clayton Alderfer, Frederick Herzberg, and John Adams; by their theories, acknowledge that subtle and variable factors affect employees' assessment of their relationships with the work processes, as well as with their employers. From their perspectives, it will seem obvious that the motivation of employees can be achieved by meeting their needs or through the designs of their jobs.

Apparently, the compensation and emoluments systems of most organizations suggest that by striving to satisfy certain needs; employees are motivated to increase their job performance. Employee motivation can, however, also be achieved through the enhancement of their perceptions of equity and expectancy. To be able to successfully guide subordinates and employees toward the intended objectives and goals, organizational leaders need to understand these psychological processes of motivation.

Motivation through Needs and Job Design

The need theories describe the motivation in organizations as being directed toward the satisfaction of the human needs that include physiological and self-fulfillment needs[5]. These need theories, as they apply to organizations, are based on various perspectives. The theories that govern motivation through the meeting of human needs and job design include Maslow's Theory of Human Motivation, Alderfer's Existence, the Relatedness, and the Growth (ERG) theory, McClelland's Need for Achievement Theory, and Frederick Herzberg's motivator-hygiene theory of Job satisfaction. As outcrops of Maslow's theories, both the Herzberg's and Alderfer's theories have close relationships.

Maslow's Theory of Human Motivation

Abraham Maslow had, in his *"theory of Human motivation"*, contended that human needs arrange themselves in hierarchies of prepotency[9]. Maslow's needs theory contends that; in an increasing order of importance, an individual has the five basic need categories: physiological needs, safety and security needs, affiliation, esteem, and self-actualization[2]. Maslow proposed that the basic and lowest human needs are those physiological needs like having enough air, water, and food to survive; the next are the safety needs that provide protection from physical and psychological harm, threats and illness; the need for affiliation that creates the desire for love, affection and interactions with other people; esteem that demands the need for reputation, and recognition, as well as prestige and self-confidence; and at the top, self-actualization that creates the desire for self-fulfillment[2].

Maslow argued that demands for these needs are arranged in steps; indicating that although we are motivated simultaneously by several needs, behaviours are influenced by the lowest unsatisfied needs. In a satisfaction-progression process; as the physiological needs are satisfied, the need for safety arises, and continues in such step-like fashion until the need for self-actualization is fulfilled.

Generally, each lower need must be satisfied before the need above it manisfests. This means that when the deficiency needs of physiology, safety, affiliation, and esteem are well satisfied, self-actualization arises. After the deficiency needs have been fulfilled, the self-actualization needs enable the individual achieve his or her real self-development; as well as offer his or her full potential to the organization. To Maslow, the self-actualizing individual is essentially a normal person who has had nothing taken away from him or her. When the individuals transcend their deficiency needs, self-actualization becomes a growth process. Creating the enabling environments for self-actualizing employees is essential for the development and well-being of both the employees and the organization. In adopting this theory, the focus of leadership in motivating employees should be on identifying and satisfying any unmet needs. Critics, however, indicate that the gratification of need level does not necessarily create an increased motivation to satisfy the higher need level[11].

In a general context, any society that substantially meets the physiological and safety needs of a large majority of its citizens; and also creates the enabling environment for their self-actualization is on its way to higher human development index levels.

Alderfer's Existence, Relatedness, and Growth (ERG) Theory

The Clayton Alderfer's Existence, Relatedness, and Growth (ERG) needs theory; which compressed Maslow's needs level from five to three needs indicates that an individual is motivated from the lowest to the highest by the Existence, the Relatedness, and the Growth (ERG) needs[2]. The Existence needs dwell on the physiological and safety needs that constitute the human basic needs necessary for existence. The Relatedness is on the desire of the individual to maintain interpersonal relationship; whereas the Growth needs are on the desire of the individual for personal development, self actualization, and self-fulfillment[8].

The Alderfer ERG theory does not, like the Maslow's theory assume a step-like progression; but rather suggests that one need can be activated seperately and at a time[8]. These three types of needs are each capable of motivating behaviors at the same time[1]. The Alferfer ERG theory also contains a frustration-regression component; as the frustration of not fulfilling a higher-order need can trigger the desire for lower-order needs[8]. If the existence and relatedness needs have been fulfilled but the growth needs remain unfulfilled, frustration sets in and relatedness needs will again regain dominance[11]. For instance, the frustration of not having self-fulfillment at job may influence the desire to form informal workplace cliches or the demand for better work conditions. Organizational leaders should, therefore, note that employees may be influenced to demand lower-order needs, such as higher pays or benefits when they are frustrated with higher-order needs, such good working environments.

Proponents indicate that the ERG theory is superior to Maslow's theory as its combination of the satisfaction-progression and frustration-regression is more explanatory of why employees need change over time[11]. Critics, however, argue that human beings inherently do not have the same needs, and that individuals prioritize their needs around their personal values. Moreover, critics argue, individuals change their need priority as their personal and social identities change[11].

McClelland's Need Theory

David McClelland's achievement need theory can also be a tool for motivational leadership. David McMClelland had, in this theory, suggested that achievement needs are important needs as they are not innate; but are rather learned, and vary from an individual to another[5]. This theory, has, over the time been elongated to three components, namely; need for achievement, need for affiliation, and need for power.

David McClelland had proposed that motivation and performance vary according to the strength of one's need for achievement[8]. This motivation model is characterized by a desire to accomplish difficult tasks, or to overcome or master human or physical obstacles, and attain high standards; as well as excel above all others. This is the motivation model for high achievers. A characteristic of individuals with high need for achievement are the preference for working on tasks of moderate difficulty; rather than challenging tasks that could lead to failure. These high needs for achievement individuals also prefer that their performances be recognized as solely the results of their efforts; rather than external factors of luck, providence, destiny, or fate. They therefore, prefer to work alone, rather than in teams.

Lastly, high achievers always desire feedbacks on their successes; as well as on their failures. Money is, however, a weak motivator for high achievement indiduals except when used as a feedback mechanism or used for recognition of achievement[11]. These individuals usually seek challenges; and therefore always try new and more efficient ways of doing things[5]. Generally, individuals with high achievement needs are not to be encouraged to the topmost leadership because such entails the need to delegate work and build support through the involvement of others[11].

The second dimension of need for affiliations takes into cognizance, the basic human desire to form and maintain lasting and positive interpersonal relationships both in personal lives and in the workplaces. Individual with high need for affiliation always seek to please others, conform to the wishes of others, and avoid confrontations and conflicts[11]. High affiliation individuals strive to project favourable images; taking steps to be liked by others. The high affiliation individuals also like to support others; trying to smooth out conflicts that occur in organizational settings. This need has been predicted as partly responsible for the desire for employees to remain with same employer[8]. Employees are usually more engaged and productive at work when they have their best friends at the workplaces[8]. Organizational leaders should therefore, encourage interpersonal relationships at workplaces.

The high affiliation individuals tend to be very effective in coordinating roles (joint/team projects); roles where cultivating long-terms relations is needed (sales and marketing), and in conflict mediations (negotiations with hostile labor unions). They are, however, less effective in areas involving the allocating resources, or in making decisions that can potentially generate conflicts[11].

The third dimension of need for power describes the individual's desire to control his or her environment that includes both personnel and material resouurces[11]. These individuals with high power needs always do want to exercise control and are always concerned with maintaining their leadership positions[11]. This need for power is also reflective of individuals who desire to influence, teach, or encourage others to achieve[8].

When individuals have the need for power, they are attracted to power-related motivation[10]. The power-need individuals like to work, and have concerns with discipline and self-respectiveness[8]. This need dimension, is however, two-faced: a positive side and a negative side. Individuals with the positive orientation focus on acomplishing group goals and helping colleagues or other employees achieve competence[8]. Conversly, the individals with negative orientation focus on winning at all costs.

Similarly, some individuals have a high need for personalized power; in which they desire power for the advancement of their carers and personal interest; while some have a high need for socialized power, as a means to help others or to improve the organization[11]. Individuals who seek personalized power, do so for the sake of power; using it as a status symbol, and for the fulfilment of personal needs[11]. Leadership positions in public organizations should be for those who seek socialized power, rather than those who seek personalized power.

Encouragingly, individuals can be trained to increase their achievement motivation. Public organizations should always organize achievement trainings for their employees. David McClelland advised that leadership be encouraged among those with higher needs for power; but not for those with high achievement motivation. On the other hand, McClelland canvassed that the level of economic development in a country relates positively to its achievement motivation[4].

Herzberg's motivator-hygiene theory of Job satisfaction

Frederick Herzberg's motivator-hygiene theory of job satisfaction was the outcome of a landmark study entitled *The Motivation to Work*[12]. The theory relates job motivation to the content and the context of the jobs. In this two-factor theory, Herzberg suggested that the factors that produce job satisfaction or motivation are different from the factors that lead to dissatisfaction[5].

The theory focuses on the outcomes that can lead to high levels of motivation and job satisfaction, called the motivators; and the outcomes that can prevent people from dissatisfaction, called the hygiene needs. The motivators are associated with the nature of work itself and are those psychological contents of the jobs; which include: achievement, recognition, responsibility, challenging work, and advancement. These are intrinsic and are similar to higher order needs that are expressed in the Maslow needs theory.

Herzberg also isolated the hygiene factors associated with job dissatisfaction, namely; company policies and administration;

32

supervision; salary; interpersonal relations, status, security, and working conditions. These are extrinsinc factors and similar to the lower needs expressed in the Maslow needs theory. Herzberg suggested that the satisfaction of these lower needs does not lead to motivation; it only leads to absence of dissatisfaction[5]. The hygiene needs have no motivational contents, but could rather prevent job dissatisfaction. It is only when the work itself is satisfying from the motivators will the employees be motivated[6].

Frederick Herzberg essentially postulated that employees experience job satifaction when their growth and esteem needs (motivators) are fulfilled; but do no experience job dissatisfaction when their other lower needs (hygiene factors) such as good working condition, job security are fulfilled[11]. The hygiene needs prevent job dissatisfaction; even when their fullfillments do not give job satisfaction.

This theory essentially deals with the factors that create satisfaction and dissatisfaction at workplaces; and those that motivate employees to higher level of performances. The motivators create high levels of job satisfaction and employee motivation; and the hygiene factors are necessary to prevent job dissatisfaction. When the hygiene needs are not met, workers dissatisfaction would increase; but satisfying those needs will not result to high levels of motivation or even high levels of job satisfaction[7]. To have a highly motivated and satisfied workforce, managers should take steps to ensure that employees' motivator needs are being met[7]. Although, the hygiene factors are not motivational; but can lead to job dissatisfaction, if absent. When, however, these hygiene factors are available in their desired forms, they are usually taken for granted[3].

One inference that can be made from Herzberg's theory of motivation is that an employee is not likely to experience job dissatisfaction if the employee has no complaints against the absence of hygiene factors. Another deduction from this theory is the consideration that Herztberg's theory seems to be of the view that the opposite of satisfaction is not dissatisfaction. The theory posits that the opposite of job dissatisfaction, is not job satisfaction, but rather no job dissatisfaction[8]. Rather, there exists the dissatisfaction-satisfaction continuum that contains a zero midpoint at which dissatisfaction and satisfaction are absent[8]. An employee who earns good salary, has good relationship with his or her supervisors, and has good working conditions (no dissatisfaction), but has boring and unchallenging tasks that create little or no chances for advancement (no satisfaction) would likely be at this zero mid-point. This Herzberg's postulation that workers are neutral toward work when they are the zero point where motivators are absent applies squarely to most public organizations.

The Herzberg theory has been found most relevant in its application to job enrichment. The concepts of job enrichment is built on modifying or re-designing a job so that an employee would have the opportunity to be so stimulated as to experience achievement, recognition, responsibility, and advancement[8]. This can be achieved through the vertical integration of responsibility. This means that rather than giving employees additional tasks of similar responsibilities (horizontal loading), organizational leaders should give subordinates additional tasks with more responsibilities (vertical loading); such as the jobs normally performed by their bosses.

On a cross-cultural and transnational perspective, an indication is that the recognition and advancement are usually strong employee motivators in most ascription cultures. As the opposite of the achievement-oriented cultures like the United States, ascription-oriented cultures are those in which status is based on such factors as birth, kinship, or interpersonal connections; rather than on personal achievement. In such cultures, such hygiene factors as salary and working conditions would not merely stop dissatisfaction, they could motivate. More so, in most developing countries in which the salaries and working conditions are poor, good salaries and good working conditions would be motivators rather than hygiene factors.

Motivation through Equity and Expectancy

The theories that govern motivation through equity and expectancy are the John Adam's Equity theory of Motivation and the Victor Vroom's expectancy theory.

Adam's Equity Theory of Motivation

The equity theories are anchored on the notion of social exchange, which suggests that individuals exert efforts to achieve goals on the basis of the assessment of the situations[5]. This model postulates that the desire for fairness and justice in social exchanges or the desire for a give-and-take relation could be a source of motivation. This model is an outcrop of the cognitive dissonance theory, which postulates that people could be motivated by the internal urge to strike consonance between their cognitive beliefs and their behaviors[8]. Employees evaluate this exchange based on what they perceive to be fair compared to what others receive or the efforts required[5]. John Adams had suggested that the individual's expectations about what is equitable are learned through social interactions and the comparison of their experiences with those of others[5].

Under the equity theory, employees do not only try to balance their efforts and rewards (ratio of inputs and outputs); they then compare it with the ratio of the inputs and outputs of other reference points; such as, their colleagues or the market place. In this comparison, it is the ratio, rather than the quantity of inputs and outputs that matters.

As this model proposes, the motivation is the consequence of perceived equitability or inequitability. The perceive inequitability creates tension that is directly proportional to the magnitude of the perceived inequality[5]. Individuals are then motivated to reduce this tension by either their input or by changing their perceptions. The postulations are that any perceived inconsistencies between beliefs and behavior would create psychological discomfort; which would, in turn, motivate corrective action[8]. Inequitability is public organizations can create counter productive behaviours; as well as increase psychological stress, absenteeism, and employee turnover rate.

The equity theory of motivation can give an understanding of how perceptions and attitudes can affect the job performance of an employee. Employees tend to become de-motivated in relationship to their jobs and employment if they perceived that the ratio of their inputs is greater than their outputs in comparison with their reference points. This can lead to the employees reacting by reducing their efforts or becoming disgruntled. The model underscores the need for a fair balance between such employee inputs as skill, hardwork,

35

tolerance, personal sacrifice, and commitment; and such outputs as salary, benefts, and recognition.

In job places, the feeling of inequity may arise when an employee feels inadequately compensated for his or her contributive inputs or has the feeling of under compensation in comparison with other persons performing similar jobs or with similar educational qualifications. The theory is therefore, primarily used to study and understand employees reaction to renumerations and compensations.

The lesson from this model is that sometimes, singling out just an employee for promotion or pay raise can have a demoralizing effect on others; as employees will likely be demotivated if they feel that they have been unfairly treated. This also model suggests that compensation and working conditions alone may not determine motivation.

Generally, employees tend to have sense of equity in organizational processes and procedures when they partake in the decision-making process[8]. Equitability in work places also promotes teamwork and cooperation among work group members. To have the right climate of equity and justice calls for a special attention on employee's perception of what is fair and equitable; especially on such issues as policies, procedures, compensations, and promotions. The job of leadership is to strive toward the reduction of inequities in the work place.

On the public or political side, the motivation that arises as a consequence of perceived inequities can be used to develop the consciousness for servant leadership. That such leaders as Martin Luther King and Mahatma Gandhi were motivated to servant leadership by the prevailing social injustices of their era are exemplifications of this motivation model.

Expectancy theory

This theory does not focus on individual needs; but rather proposes that people are motivated when they expect that their efforts will result to desirable outcomes[5]. The expectancy theory of motivation anchors on the postulation that individuals are motivated by the desire to act in ways that would produce the expected outcomes[8]. The theory proposes that work effort is directed toward the behaviors that people believe and expect to produce the desired outcomes[11].

The theory also suggest that if individuals believe they possess the needed skills and abilities; that their hard work will result in high performances; that they would be rewarded and want the rewards; then they are more likely to exert the needed efforts[5]. The argument is that if any of these factors are absent, motivation will be adversely affected. For instance, if individuals do not believe that their efforts will be rewarded, they are not likely to put in much effort.

The expectancy theory indicates that the motivation to exert effort increases as one's "effort-performance-outcome" expectations improve[8]. Perception is very pivotal as the theory emphasizes the cognitive ability to anticipate likely outcomes of behaviors or choices. What does the individual expect when he or she makes the decision of whether to stay or quit a job? What does the individual expect when he or she makes the decision of whether to major in engineering, computer science, or physics?

Victor Vroom in a book, *Work and Motivation* had argued that it is the strength of the individual's desire for a particular outcome, and the association that individual makes between actions and outcomes that create motivation[13]. The motivation arises from the decision of how much effort to exert on particular tasks[8]. The expectancy component is the belief (or expectation) of the individual that a particular level of efforts will produce a particular level of performance. The motivation is then influenced by the perceived potentiality (or expectation) of getting particular outcomes as the result of accomplishing particular performance goals. Expectancy is zero when there is an indication that there is no anticipation that the efforts would have any impact on performance. Hence, choosing rewards and outcomes that match the worker and linking handwork to reward enhances motivation.

Under this theory, the level of effort put in by an employee is determined by both the expectancy placed on certain outcomes (rewards) and the degree to which people belief that their efforts will lead to the rewards[5]. The efforts may, however, not always lead to task accomplishment even when the employee is highly motivated. To achieve accomplishments when motivated, organizations must consider employee ability, as well as role clarity. A motivated employee must also possess the ability to perform the task; as well as the understanding of how to direct efforts in manners that align with the person's organizational role[5]. In summary, the expectancy theories suggests the following of employees: (i) employees believe that they possess the needed skills and abilities, (ii) employees believe their hardwork will result in good performances, (iii) that their performances will be rewarded, (iv) that they want the reward, and then (v) they are more likely to exert the required efforts[5]. If any of these factors is absent, motivation is likely to be absent too.

The expectancy theory, therefore, portends that employees think about the expected payoffs for their efforts; as well as the opportunities, rewards, and the incentives that exist in the work environment[5]. Secondly, as different individuals have different abilities and skills, they are more likely to exert more efforts in those areas where they believe they are more likely to perform well[5]. To enhance motivation, leaders should choose the rewards or outcomes that are of value to a particular employee or group of employees[5]. Leaders can also work to alter the expectancy of existing perceptions in such manners as to strengthen the link between hardwork and reward[5]. The factors that could improve an employee's expectancy perception include; self-esteem, self-efficacy, and previous success at tasks; assistance from bosses and subordinates; as well as the availability of the information, materials, and equipment necessary to complete the tasks. The job of the leader becomes that of ensuring that these positive factors are available.

PATH II

THEORIES and CONCEPTS of LEADERSHIP in PUBLIC ORGANIZATIONS

Chapter 7

Classical Theories of Leadership

The process of influencing people to direct their efforts toward the achievement of some particular goal or performance is leadership[4]. Leadership skills can also be described as the ability to use and influence effectively; the ability to communicate with and motivate others; and the ability to work in and among diverse groups[2]. In both private and public organizations, leaders often use their powers to affect the behavior and performance of the subordinates. There exists a natural necessity for leadership in all societies; as it is essential to the functions of all organizations within the societies.

Leadership Theories (The Classics)

Although leadership theories have not adequately addressed the nature and challenges of leadership; some earlier scholars had, over the years, canvassed various theories; all in the quest to explain human leadership behaviors and styles. Such classical theories are the trait, behavioral, and contigency (situational) theories of leadership.

The traits theory

The trait theory postulates that leadership is the set of exemplary traits, values, and behaviors that individuals do possess[11]. This trait approach to leadership summarizes the old concept or saying that leaders are born and not made; which presupposes that certain traits are inherent in leaders. This theory also projects leaders as generally more intelligent, more dependable, and more socially active than non-leaders[2]. As the traits associated with leadership vary from culture to culture, and also from time to time; it can be deduced, from this perspective, that leadership traits are variable[2].

Arguments against this perspective of leadership include that leadership does not depend on the possession of certain traits, but rather through a relationship between the leader and members of the group[10]. Moreover, although a few traits are consistently associated with effective leaders, most are, however, unrelated to effective leadership[10]. Also, with true and dedicated efforts, such leadership skills as transformational leadership can be learned[1].

The Behavioral Theories

The behavioral theory of leadership seeks to explain the relationship between leadership effectiveness and human relations for which the trait theory could not account for[8]. The theory focuses on the leader's behavior rather than on the leader's personality traits. The main competences of this model are the leadership behaviors associated with creating mutual respect and concerns for the needs and desires of the followers; and with what should be done to maximize output[8]. For instance, leaders with strong people-oriented styles would listen to followers, do personal favors to followers, support their interest when required, and treat them as equals[9].

Contingency (Situational) Theories

The situational leadership theories are meant to address the inconsistencies of the traits and behavioral theories by positing that the effectiveness of a particular leadership behavior is dependent on the prevailing situations[8]. This belief that leadership style changes with situation creates the impression that there is no best style of leadership. The models for the situational leadership include; Fiedler's contingency model, the path-goal theory, and Hersey-Blanchard's model.

Fiedler's contingency model

This situational model, developed by Fred Fiedler is the oldest and most widely acknowledged model of situational leadership[8]. In the epic article titled, *Job Engineering for Effective Leadership: A new approach*, Fred Fiedler posited that the effectiveness of a group is contingent on the relationship between the style of leadership and the degree to which the situation enables the leader to exert influence[2].

According to Fred Fiedler, the effectiveness of a leader is

dependent on the basic motivation of the leader and the degree to which the situation gives the leader control and influence[3]. From this perpective, leadership can be analyzed from the ability to influence action and motivation based on the situational contexts and follower characteristics[11]. Most political leaderships are not only situational; but are also based on this contingency model. It could, therefore, be presupposed that the "greatness" of leaders arises from the existence of the "enabling environment."

Path-Goal theory

The path-goal theory developed by Robert House is anchored on the expectancy theory of motivation[6]. Robert House postulated that effective organizational leaders influence employees' performance by making their need satisfaction dependent on effective job performance[9]. This leadership model canvasses that leadership effectiveness is influenced by interaction between directive, supportive, participative, and achievement-oriented leadership style; and such contingency factors as followership characteristics and the environment[8]. The well informed and confident followers would most likely prefer participative or achievement-oriented leadership; whereas ill-informed followers or those that lack self-confidence are more likely to embrace supportive or directive leadership[9]. Effective leaders therefore, strengthen the effort-to-performance expectancy by ensuring that employees have the information, support, and the resources they need to perform their duties[7].

Hersey-Blanchard's Theory

In the book, *Management of Organizational Behavior*, one of the pioneering works on situational leadership, Paul Hersey and Kenneth Blanchard[5] postulated that leadership is the process of influencing the activities of individuals or groups toward goal development and achievement; under given situations. The situational leadership theory of Paul Hersey and Kenneth Blanchard is hinged on the postulation that effective leadership behaviors are dependent on the extent to which followers possess both the ability and the willingness (the readiness level of the followers)[5]. The performance of the leader is enhanced as the readiness level of the followers increase. These theorists postulate that increasing leadership behavior from the lower level of providing instructions, to selling and explaining; to followers' participation, and then to delegating responsibilities; would gradually increase the readiness level of the followers.

Chapter 8

New Perspectives of Leadership

The most discussed of the new perspectives to leadership theories are the charismatic, transactional, transformational, and servant leadership styles[22]. At their introduction into political discussions by the political scientist, James McGregor Burns, he had suggested a ditchotomy between transactional and transformational leadership; describing both as ends of a leadership continuum[6]. Bernard Bass in the book, *Leadership and Performance beyond Expectations*, however, outlines a theory of leadership in which both transactional and tranformational are not the opposite ends to a continuum, but are rather leadership patterns possessed by leaders; and can be used in varying quantities[4]. Bernard Bass argued that the best performance can be found in the use of the two leadership behaviors. The "full range" leadership theory of Bernard Bass breaks leadership behaviour into eight operational modes: laissez-faire, passive management by exception, active management by exception, contingent reward, individualized consideration, idealized influence, intellectual stimulation, and inspirational motivation[26].

Modern Leadership Models

The new perspectives to leadership perceive it as a system of interacting inputs, processes, outputs, and feedback; that desire meaningful direction and purpose from the performance system and environment within which leadership occurs[24]. The phenomenon of leadership, hence, comes with the need to achieve the goals desired by the internal and external stakeholders of a specific performance system[24]. The new leadership approaches require communicating goals, roles, and responsibilities; inspiring confidence in leadership direction and resources, resolving issues, and delivering results[17]. As leadership conceptualizes the future and aligns goals with the common vision, it provides the inspirations needed to achieve transformational goals[16]. These perspectives tend to give credence to the contingency approach to leadership. On another hand, an authentic leader only builds people through service by putting people first; and viewing and treating them with dignity and respect[29]. More so, the primary characteristic of most of the leaders who have made positive contributions to mankind is humility[9]. These last two perspectives tend to support the servant leadership model.

Charismatic Leadership

The concept of charismatic leadership is the foundation for most of the modern theories of leadership. A leader is charismatic on the basis of the possession of such characteristics that inspire and direct followers by building the commitment to shared vision and values[13]. Charismatic leadership is the theoretical underpinnings for transformational and servant leadership paradigms[22]. The idealized influence aspect of transformational leadership is very close to charismatic leadership[6]. Acknowledging that charismatic leadership is a component of transformational leadership means that a leader may be charismatic, and yet not transformational. In making a distinction between charismatic and transformational leadership; there is another distinction: whereas charimatic leaders often create new institutions, movements, or organizations; transformational leaders tend to change existing ones[25].

Transactional Leadership

This leadership approach involves the exchange of value between initiators and respondents[11]. Transactional leadership is essentially a process of social exchange between followers and leaders; involving reward-based transactions[22]. The transactional leaders (sometimes called simply management) are individuals who exchange rewards for efforts and performance; and who tend to lead on a 'something for something" basis. The rewards are for the purposes of meeting the goals and expectations that have been set for the followers or subordinates[22].

Transactional leadership can also be essentially considered as a networking of power[21]. Transactional leadership manifests in different forms. These include contingent reward leadership, active or passive management-by-exception, or laissez leadership[5].

Usually, transactional leaders indicate the specific rewards for accomplishing agreed-upon tasks. Transactional leadership style involves negotiations between leaders and their subordinates; and the exchange of relationships between them. In the transactional leadership model, two parties engage in a relationship that advances mutual interests without any deep or enduring link between them[11]. These leaders practice the traditional management function of leading, and usually have a sense of commitment that tends more to the organization; and they also tend to conform to organizational norms and values.

The transactional leader creates clarification for performance expectations, and goals; and the paths that link performance to rewards[22]. They use contingent reward considerations when setting up transactions with followers for the purposes of rewarding for achieved work goals[4]. To do this, the transactional leader monitors followers' performance and creates corrective actions whenever necessary[6]. Transaction leadership draws support from the postulation that a strong leadership breeds a strong and appropriate organizational behavior, which in turn, enhances job performance; whereas a weak or bad leadership creates an opposite result[1].

Transformational Leadership

James MacGregor Burns in a classical study, titled *Leadership,* developed this key leadership concept that captures the dynamics of meeting goals[11]. This concept cuts across cultures and time; and focuses on the relationship between leaders and followers[11]. The transformational approach to leadership addresses the limitations of both the traits and situational perspectives by isolating sets of behaviors that can produce positive results in many different contexts[14].

Transformational leadership arises when a leader inspires and shares a vision with followers; and empowers followers toward achieving the vision[22]. Transformational leadership evolves as leaders and followers engage with one another in such a manner that raises one another to higher levels of morality and motivation[11]. This leadership then grows out of a sense of the vision and energy received from the leader[27].

These leaders are usually charismatic; and can elevate the consciousness of subordinates about new outcomes; motivating them to transcend their own interests for the sake of the organization[10]. Transformation leadership emphasizes the higher order needs of followers that include "esteem, competency, self-fulfillment, and self-actualization[14]. Another major attribute of this leadership is that it usually creates a clear, compelling, and energizing vision that serves as a unifying focal point of efforts; thereby creating strength when there seem to be weakness; and courage when there seems to be cowardice[3]. Transformational leaders focus on arousing the consciousness of followers by appealing to such higher ideals and moral values as liberty, justice, equality, peace, and humanitarianism[6].

This form of leadership usually rests on a clear ethical foundation. The goal of a transforming leader is essentially to raise the level of morality in a group or organization[14]. The moral and ethical responsibilities of transformation leadership starkly differentiate this leadership style from those preceding it, such as transactional leadership[14]. As transformational leadership consists of a set of practices, then anyone can function as a transformational leader by adopting these behaviors[14].

Bernard Bass, in the "full range" leadership theory stated the four main characteristics of transformational leadership as: idealized influence (charisma), inspirational motivation, intellectual stimulation, and individualized consideration[2]. The idealized influence, which is also a component of charismatic leadership, is that in which the leader directs and inspires followers by building the commitment to shared vision and values. The intellectual simulation arises from those behaviors of the leader which encourage creativity and stimulate innovativeness within the followers[22]. Individualized consideration is the ability of the leader to develop the potentials of the followers; and at same time, paying attention to their individual needs for growth and achievement[22]. The individualized consideration, idealized influence, intellectual stimulation, and inspirational motivation in which followers perceived personalized support; sense of vision; role model, and stimulation to change are the key elements of transformational leadership[26]. The theory of transformational model is a normative form of leadership and an important precursor to servant leadership, which is also another form of normative leadership.

Servant Leadership

The term "servant leadership" was first conceptualized by Robert Greenleaf, a former AT&T employee, and founder of Greenleaf Center for Servant Leadership. He described servant leadership as a leadership model that puts the concerns of followers at the forefront[14]. Servant leaders are altruistic, simplistic, self-awarded, and morally sensitive with motives of actions. They are characterized by the four central concepts of stewardship, obligation, partnership, and elevating purpose[14]. Some scholars have, however, expanded the characteristics of servant leadership to six components: valuing people, developing people, building communities, displaying authenticity, providing leadership, and sharing leadership[18]. Some other scholars have also argued that such components of transformational leadership as idealized influences, inspirational motivation and individualized consideration are also components of the servant leadership[23].

As Greenleaf noted, a servant leader leads because he or she wants to serve others[7]. The goal of a servant leader is to help his or her followers grow and develop as productive members of society[14]. In its genuine form, this leadership style tends to create less potential for leaders to take advantage of the trust of followers; or the undue accumulation of wealth and power[14]. Any leadership style that places the good of the led over the self-interest of the leader encapsulates servant leadership.

Other New Leadership Models

Post-Industrial Leadership

This leadership model was developed by James Rost, who had contended that most other leadership models are anchored on the industrial era perception of leaders as "super managers" who set goals; and from various perspectives make followers achieve the desired objectives[20]. On the contrary, the post-industrial leadership model demands putting greater value on collaboration, consensus, diversity, and participation[20]. In this leadership concept, leaders, and followers set and pursue common good in a two-way flow of influence[29]. The relationship focuses on persuasion rather that coercion; with influence following both ways as ethical standards develop in the process of the interrelationships[29].

James Rost laid out the four key elements of postindustrial leadership as: (i) relationships that thrive on multiplicity of influences; with leaders influencing followers, followers influencing leaders, and followers influencing followers; (ii) leaders and followers as active partners with both forming one relationship called leadership; (iii) leaders and followers intending and designing purposeful and substantial changes focusing on making significant differences in the lives individuals, groups, organizations and societies; and (iv) leaders and followers developing mutual purposes that allow them create communities[20].

Arguments have been made on the superiority of post-industrial leadership over transformational leadership. James Rost had posited that post-industrial leadership is superior because it focuses on the relationship between leaders and followers; rather than exalting the leaders over the followers[20]. James Rost also insisted that other leadership concepts downplay this leader-follower relationship; and rather require leaders to use followers to achieve the goals the leaders have set themselves[20].

Authentic Leadership

This leadership concept is hinged on the ancient Greek philosophy: to thine own self be true[12]. Fred Luthans and Bruce Avolio who developed this concept of leadership portrayed it as a process by which leaders are deeply aware of how they think and behave; the context of their operation as perceived by others; and the awareness of their values and those of others[8]. Authentic leadership is a higher order leadership concept that creates self-awareness, relational transparency; and the internal appreciation of moral and ethical values[28]. This approach is a shift of the perspectives of leadership from the traditional assumption of leadership that had focused on the behaviors of leaders only; but not on the behaviors of the followers[8].

An effective model of authentic leadership is a two-way model that canvasses that judgments about the leader should not only be analyzed on the basis of what the leader has done; but also on what the followers have attributed to the leader, and vice versa[12]. Authentic leadership, therefore, draws on awareness, unbiased processing, action, and relational relationship[15].

When Fred Luthans and Bruce Avolio first proposed the concept of authentic leadership, they had argued that issues of today have made it unquestionably necessary for leaders to be transparent, value-oriented, and to develop ethical perspective to leadership. Under this leadership concept, leaders are concerned, not only with their personal authenticity, but also on how the authenticity can be conveyed to followers as an instrument of influence toward common goals, objectives, or aspirations[8]. Positive outcomes can only emerge from authentic leadership when followers perceive leaders as authentic[8]. The primary argument here is that the perceptions followers have of their leaders are far more influential in determining follower behavior[19]. This leadership model, therefore, involves a more integrative approach to the analysis of leadership and organizational behavior[12]. There are strong suggestions to conclude that authentic leadership is the major concept at the foundation of transformational leadership.

Chapter 9

Models for Normative Leaderships

Normative leadership deals with how leaders ought to behave; based on moral principles or norms[13]. The transformational and servant leadership models are both forms of normative leadership. Transformational leadership inspires followers to share a vision; empowering them to achieve the vision; and also provides the resource necessary for developing their personal potential[19]. Servant leadership is the model in which the leader views himself as a servant to those he leads, and elevates the interest of followers before the self-interest of a leader; and also emphasizes personal development and empowerment of followers[19]. Both leadership styles are from the mould of charismatic leadership style in which leaders wield power by virtue of the identification and belief in the leader by the followers[26]. The transformational and servant leadership models have brought new ideas of leadership into the mainstream; and have changed the way institutions, including the long-lasting ones, handle leader-follower relationships.

Transformational Leadership Model

Transformational leadership occurs when leaders and followers engage with one another in such a way that they elevate one another to higher levels of morality and motivation[8]. Transformational leaders accomplish this by motivating people; and showing them how their role is significant within the context of the larger operation. They also focus on an individual's strengths; inspiring the individual to tap into his or her creative reserves; in order to arrive at something compelling, meaningful, and satisfying. Obviously, transformational leaders tend to trust subordinates; and then, earn their trust in return.

A leader using the transformational strategies has the specific goal of elevating the level of morality of both the followers and the organization; creating a more moral climate, fostering independent action, and serving the greater good[27]. This leadership style adds to the quality of life in people and organizations by appealing to higher ideals[18].

Transformational leadership offers leadership through its conscious efforts to develop the needs of its followers from lower to higher levels of maturity[2]. This it does, by appealing and motivating followers to higher ideals and moral values; articulating visions that are hinged on the foundations of credibility[22]. Although, we do understand that transformational leadership is a form that demonstrates extreme charisma; it also motivates employees and subordinates to transcend their personal interests for the good of the group or organization[4]. The transformational approach isolates a learned set of behaviors; and this has proved successful in producing positive results in different contexts[13].

Transformational leaders emphasize the personal development and empowerment of followers, by facilitating a shared vision and placing their interests at the top of the agenda[19]. The leader provides the necessary resources for the development and achievement of personal potential[19]. Transformational leaders also focus on terminal values like liberty, equality, and justice. These values mobilize and energize followers; as well as create an agenda for action and appeal to larger audiences[13]. Transformational leadership, not only inspires followers to share a vision, but also empowers and provides the resource necessary for the development of the vision. The transformational leaders are like coaches; striving to motivate and role-model followers; who admire, respect and trust them.

Under a transformational leadership model, there is the similarity between leader and follower; which exerts positive influence on the relationship and on the outcomes[10]. The existence of this positive relationship supports mutual acceptance and understanding; which would in turn; serve as an important foundation for successful cooperation[10]. A dissonance would, however, create a greater need for negotiation; thereby reducing positive assessments and efficiency[10].

This leadership model demands a higher morality and ethical reasoning than some of the other leadership styles, including the servant leadership. This is because servant leaders make conscious efforts to increase morality levels in their organizations and among the people who follow them[13]. This model enables the leaders form moral relationships with their followers that could transform both the leader and the followers. These moral and ethical responsibilities of transformation leadership differentiate this leadership style from the non-normative styles of leadership. For a public organization, an advantage of having a transformational leader is that he or she can create an ethical climate that raises the awareness of the moral standards in the workplace.

Servant Leadership Model

The tenet of servant leadership is anchored on putting the needs of the followers before those of the leader. The strength of leadership style lies on concern for others, simplicity, and the desire to serve; listening to theirs; as well as on moral sensitivity[13]. Servant leadership puts primary focus on the needs of the followers before the needs of the leader[27]. In order to be effective, servant leadership, as an extension of participative leadership, must involve the three key levels of: observing what people do, influencing what they think, and tapping into common feelings and values. Hence, servant leaders usually make efforts to pulse the feelings of their followers; re-adjusting their strategies accordingly[7].

The initiator of servant leadership model, Robert Greenleaf had suggested that servant leaders are not initially motivated to lead; but become involved by the prodding of others; and for the sake of group's success. With its unique motivation, servant leadership may create a different type of organizational culture[19]. More so, as the servant leader is more likely to gain the trust of others and those they supervise by acting consistently; and also by avoiding the typical traps of other types of leaderships that display more ambiguous moral standards and relative ethics[13].

As the concern for others comes before concern for self, altruism is the first strength of servant leadership; whereas simplicity is the second. Self-awareness is the third strength of servant leadership as they listen to themselves, as well as to others; taking time for reflection, and recognizing the importance of spiritual resources[13]. The servant leader therefore, has to possess such skills as listening receptively, persuading, and communicating effectively[20]. Moral sensitivity is the fourth strength of servant leadership as they are acutely aware of the importance of pursuing the ethical purposes that bring meaning and fulfillment to work[13].

As a servant leader is motivated by the desire to serve, he or she is eager to provide resources and support without the expectation of acknowledgement[19]. A servant leader places the good of those who are led ahead of self-interest; viewing followers as partners, and not as subordinates[13]. A servant leader understands the needs of the master (the followers) because they endeavor to hear, see, know, and have exceptional intuitive insight[12].

In practice, the characteristic behaviors of a servant leader include; selflessness, promotion of self-awareness among their followers, and the incorporation of moral sensitivity. This leadership is seen as an opportunity to serve others and develop the full potentials of individuals; so that the society can benefit as well. Servant leadership demonstrates concerns for the welfare and development of followers, influencing their followers through personal development and empowerment[25].

The other significant characteristics of a servant leader are those of healing, persuasion, foresight, commitment to people, and community building[5]. As servant leaders are great listeners, this talent requires connecting with one's own inner voice in a manner that will enable the individual comprehend and communicate much more effectively. With the foresight and commitment to the people, the servant leader usually possesses a long-term approach to life and work; as they relate to the systematic processes of implementing positive changes in society. As putting others' needs first is something they should do, and they should also judged by what happens in their follower's life[13].

In the service of the public and in public entities, an advantage of using the servant leadership style is that it leaves less potential for corruption and naked abuse of power[13]. This leadership paradigm articulates principles that shape both individual and organizational behavior.

The servant leadership model, has however, been criticized as seemingly unrealistic, may not work in every situation or organization, or could pose a danger of being used to serve the wrong cause. It has also been tagged as a concept of weakness that is not reflective of the egocentric and assertive nature of man[27]. The altruistic, simplistic, and moral sensitivity tendencies of the servant leaders are sometimes, perceived as unrealistic traits that are associable with passivity or weakness[13].

Comparisons of Normative Leadership
Similarities
The normative theories of transformation and servant leaderships bear some resemblance to each other; as both employ moral standards and values when implementing and exhibiting leadership characteristics. While there are theoretical differences between these styles of leadership, they are similar as both styles include aspects of respect, trust, integrity, and vision[25]. Both styles involve the appreciation and consideration of their followers; and both styles encourage innovation and creativity[25]. They are also quite similar in their pursuit of higher order appeals to their followers and their emphasis on the moral element of leadership[13]. Despite any differences both transformational and servant leadership styles are not only charismatic, but also have other overlapping and similar attributes[19].

The most striking similarities between servant and transformation leadership are the emphasis on individualized appreciation and consideration of followers[21]. Based on Bernard Bass's "full range" theory, there exists a componential overlap of idealized influences, inspirational motivation, and individualized consideration between servant and transformational leadership[21]. Like transformational leadership, servant leadership strives to raise the moral level of the organization or society[13]. Essentially, transformational model is 70% positively related to servant leadership[25].

They are also similar in that they are non-traditional leadership models and both are interested in improving the morale of individuals within the organization. In both styles of leadership the leaders emphasize moral character and ethical behavior; as the leaders are thought and expected to act with good moral character; as well as make ethical decisions. They are required to make decisions that will progress the group as a whole and not detrimental to it. In both models, the focus is on the overall welfare of the group as the most important goal or vision. It is the pathway to the realization of the goals that differentiates them. Arising from these similarities, it could be said that servant leadership is a sub-style within the overarching theory of transformation leadership.

Differences

The transformational leadership model theory suggests that the leaders appeal to a much larger segment of the general population and are inspirational; whereas servant model theory promulgates altruistic tendencies and suggests leading by example[13]. Servant leadership is considered to be a radical shift from transformational leadership because of its emphasis on leaders serving followers as opposed to the opposite[6]. On the other hand, leaders that demonstrate transformative methods often use conflict situations to elevate subordinates and rarely dilute their morals and value base to build consensus[6].

Although the servant leadership style is similar to the transformational leadership style, they differ as the servant seeks more to satisfy the needs of the follower. A servant leader understands the needs of the subordinates as he or she listens and pays attention to them; unlike the transformational leaders who engage in participation with the followers; rather than just listen.

Servant leadership style also differs from the transformational leadership style as the relationships are not reciprocal; as the servant leader has no voice. The leader in this servant leadership relationship is the servant and the followers are the master. Under the servant leadership model, the leaders' motivation to lead arises from an underlying and innate attitude to egalitarianism[19].

Another differentiating context of servant leadership is that members have equal rights to vision, respect, and information; with the belief that the leader knows no better than those of the led[19]. The leader's role is that of a trustee; and the growth and development of the individual are the goals. In contrast, the transformational leader emerges from the different motivation base of a sense of mission for creating survivalist measures to internal and external challenges[19].

Another major difference between the two styles can also be found in the differing ways the leaderships view their followers. Transformational leadership strongly emphasizes the integrity of followers, yet still acknowledges a somewhat subordinate relationship between leader and follower; whereas servant leadership sees followers and leaders as partners[13]. Obviously, even as transformational and servant are both moral and inspirational, they differ for the reason that servant leadership allows for more passive followers[11].

A transformational leader develops the vision and carries followers along; whereas the servant leader functions as an agent of the followers who have entrusted them with duties and opportunities for a limited time[13]. Transformational leaders are usually a source of charisma and enjoy the admiration of their followers; which usually develops to "personality worshipping". Conversely, servant leadership discourages any tendencies of "personalized idolization".

Although the high calls for ethical standards and concern for others exist in both styles, they exist for different reasons[19]. In servant leadership, high ethical standards arise from the belief in human dignity; whereas in transformation leaderships they exist because of the need to create "virtuous" foundations[19].

As a leader plays a critical role in creating an organization's culture, a servant leadership leads to a spiritual generative culture; while transformational leadership leads to an empowered dynamic culture[19]. The spiritual generative culture is that in which organizational members focus on the personal growth of themselves, other members, as well as the organization that facilitates the growth[19]. With empowered dynamic culture, members have high expectations placed upon them[19].

Classic components of transformational leadership are that the members of the group willingly make sacrifices for the leader's vision to come to fruition; and in return, the leader shows such traits as dedication, a strong sense of purpose and perseverance, and confidence in the purpose of the group. A transformational leader is able to move followers beyond their self-interests for the good of the group. On the contrary, servant leadership entails the leader being self sacrificial in order for the needs of the group to be met. They are more concerned with the overall welfare and increase in the standard of living for the group members than comfort of self. They invoke such emotions as empathy and care; and are thought to be born for this form of leadership[15].

Where transformation leadership is an active process in which the leader is creating an environment in which both leaders and followers work together to motivate; servant leadership has drawn criticism due to the perception that it is a passive style of leadership[13]. The tendency of the followers of a transformational leader to assimilate the leader's values and faults is contrary to servant leadership style in which the leader of the group takes on more of a selfless role and leads by doing what is best for the group, while putting self last.

Another difference between transformational leadership and servant leadership concepts is based on the focus of the leader. The servant leaders focus on people; with the primary emphasis on service, rather than organizational results[21]. As the servant leader focuses on the followers, the achievement of organizational objectives becomes a subordinate outcome. With the transformational leadership, the focus is directed toward the organization; with his or her behavior aimed at building follower commitment toward organizational objectives. The transformational leader focuses on organizational results; believing that the fortunes of the individuals should be tied to the fortunes of the organization[19]. This extent, to which the leader is able to shift the primary focus of leadership from the organization to the follower is also a distinguishing factor in classifying leaders as either transformational or servant leaders.

Servant leadership could be seen as passive leadership if viewed through the full spectrum of leadership model and has drawn criticism due to this perception of passivity[13]. Transformational leadership is aggressive and more rigorously structured, while servant leadership are the meek at heart.

Despite that both transformational and servant leadership styles are linked to the charismatic leadership style and also have overlapping and similar attributes, they are very different, especially with regard to the best application of each[19]. In leading public organizations, the transformation leadership concept suits an environment in which employees are given greater responsibility, encouraged to innovate, and molded to take initiative and risk[19]. On the other hand, servant leadership fits in better in nonprofit, religious, and volunteer agencies[19]. Essentially, transformation leadership is best suited for an environment requiring innovation or change; and a servant leader best suited in non-profit organizations, religious, advocacy, passive resistance, and volunteer environments.

In the life stages of a public organization, the transformational leadership will be needed at the formative, turbulent, crisis point of a public organization, or at any declining stage; when the organization would need to undergo structural changes. The servant leadership is needed at the maturity stage when the concerns for employees' personal growth are higher. Hence, both can complement each other; especially from the aspect of organizational transformation.

In most cases, servant leadership is driven by the need for social change and rectifying societal ills. In the social and political contexts, servant leaders are humble people who, for greater good, are willing to endure harrassments and incarcerations in order to bring about change for the group, as examplified by Mathama Ghandi, Dr Martin Luther King, Jr, and Nelson Mandela. Transformational leaders as examplifiied by John F.Kennedy, Lyndon Johnson, and Barack Obama, are driven by goals and meeting expectations; doing so in an innovative and creative manners.

Challenges of Normative Leadership

The perils of leadership manifest when leaders allow their "darkside" to reign and become more concerned in converting for personal gains, the resources that the people or the state provide; rather than offering services to the people. Power becomes a potential danger if leaders focus on themselves alone rather that serving the people[3]. Although, the transformational and servant leadership models are both valuable forms of leadership; both have their ethical challenges, as they both walk a thin ethical line.

The five potential forms of darkened leadership are (i) the compulsive leader who is status conscious and tries to perfect everything for the sake of gaining approval, (ii) the narcissistic leader who tries to succeed to gain admiration, (ii) the paranoid leader who is suspicious, hostile, and insecure, (iv) the co-dependent leader who takes on more than necessary and suppresses emotions and problems, and (v) the passive-aggressive leader who is stubborn, complaining, angry, sad, and manipulative[16]. In addition, leaders who lack integrity can rely upon deceit and manipulation to encourage people to follow their agenda[23].

Notwithstanding that the motivation for leadership could be noble and well meaning; a leadership model could be adversely affected and grossly impaired if it acquires a dark side. Obviously, behaviors and tendencies could cast dark shadows on those positive models of leadership. As all leaders possess some measure of positive and negative factors, by creating, monitoring, and maintaining accountability, leaders are curtailed from nurturing their dark side[3]. Hence, despite these challenges, the well-practiced cases of transformational and servant leaderships have produced amazing results.

Challenges of transformational leadership

The transformational leadership model does have its own downside. When transformational leaders do not rely upon strong ethical and moral foundation, problem could arise[23]. Although, the transformational leader is effective in instilling vision, the results might be unsettling if such visions are flawed[17]. For instance, to promote their own interest, transformational leaders often downplay the contributions of the followers[14].

Another potential danger of transformational leadership is the rise of a cult leader[3]. A cult leader tries to change the world to fit his or her image, appealing to needs of the followers; but employing charisma and other methods to charm (fool) followers into doing anything for him or her[3]. This kind of leadership can lead to follower manipulation for the purposes of the leader's interest, rather than the interest of the followers[27]. On this basis, a distinction could be made between transformational and pseudo-transformational leaders; with the latter been self-centered and manipulative; whereas the transformational leader's motivation has altruistic inclinations[1]. The most serious potential weakness of transformational is therefore, its potentialities of been used for immoral ends[27].

Transformational leadership has been criticized as been leader-centric, as the direction of the group is determined and focused on the person who is in the position of leadership or authority; and so individual's efforts are unaccounted for[13]. Typical implications of this leadership style include; environments in which followers or subordinates respect, admire, and trust the leader and emulate his or her behavior, assume his or her values[24]. The followers tend to assimilate the leader's values and faults; subject to their vision for the group. Subordinates then tend to become increasing more dependent on the leader[13].

In public organizations, this disadvantage could create over dependency of the employees and subordinates; making the organization leader-centric. To control and overcome the inner temptations to manipulate, as well as reduce the external pressures to compromise, further safeguards are needed[27]. Afterall, the transformational leadership defined by James Burns requires moral and ethical components to leadership behavior[13]. Hence, to be perceived as genuine, transformational leadership must be hinged on moral character, ethical values, and the morality of the process[23].

Challenges of servant leadership

Servant leadership, in contrast, has the potential for manipulation of the leader; as a leader's sacrifices and earnest commitment may potentially be misconstrued; thus lessening his or her ability to leader. Another challenge of this leadership approach is that it may not work in every context as it is considered to be unattainable in modern work environments. Such criticisms can, however, be seen as the normal reactions to a concept that not only differs, but also threatens those that wield or seek power in hierarchical structures[9].

PATH III

LEADERSHIP MODELS for PUBLIC ORGANIZATIONS

Chapter 10

Transactional Leadership: Model for Bureaucracies

Transactional leadership is the most basic form of leadership as it focuses on meeting the basic needs of followers. Transactional leadership hinges on the bureaucratic and organizational standards[8], and is akin to a manager of planning and policy[4]. Transactional leaders practice the traditional management function of leading, usually have a sense of commitment to the organization, and tend to conform to organizational norms and values. Obviously, the top-down, and command-and-control styles of management seem to be implicit in transactional leadership. The transactional leadership relies and thrives on existing organizational structures[6]. Hence, it depends on the power and authority structures that exist in the organizations[1].

Transactional leaders focus on the allocation of resources; and the monitoring and control of followers for the purposes of achieving organizational goals[3]. The transactional leader requires the use of rewards, sanctions, and formal authority to induce compliance[9]. The key element of transactional leadership is contingent rewarding in which leaders use performance evaluation and reward to motivate[7]. To reward performances, the transaction leader monitors the performance of the followers and takes corrective actions whenever mistakes are made. Transactional leadership is widely used in organizations with hierarchical structures as is obtainable in most public organizations.

The passive management by exception and laissez faire leadership competences of the transactional leadership model relates negatively to the servant leadership model[19]. It is, however, possible for transaction leaders to share decision-making and consider the interest of the followers when determining the exchange of the rewards for compliance[9]. Hence, when developing and using the contingent reward competence, the transactional leader can still introduce an element of servant leadership by creating work expectations that have been mutually agreed upon.

In comparing transactional leadership to transformational leadership in government and public organizations, it is worthy to state that both models are important. Using Bernard Bass's leadership model and the impact of its eight competences on employee satisfaction, it would be noted that the lower-level factors, namely; contingent reward, passive management by exception, and active management by exception, are characteristics of transactional leadership. On the other hand, the higher-level factors, namely; individualized consideration, idealized influence, intellectual stimulation, and inspirational motivation, all characterize transformational leadership. Recently, this kind of leadership has become common in the United States as managers now accept that to motivate workers, it is necessary to satisfy their higher order needs[2].

In the United State's government machineries, the applications of both transactional and transformational leaderships are regarded as important; although the latter is slightly more important[7]. For the purposes of exceptional performance, the transformational leadership behaviors need to augment the transactional leadership behaviors that currently exist within the system[7]. Thus, public organizations can be more effective with a combination of transactional and transformational leadership. To build the high-performing transformational competences in public organizations, the contingent reward, and active management by exception (transactional competences), should be in place[7]. Accordingly, the best results can be achieved by deploying both the transformational and transactional behavioral concepts in dealings with subordinates and employees.

Although, both transformational and transactional leadership are at the opposite ends of the leadership theory continuum; but rather than been antagonistic as previously perceived, transformational and transactional leadership behaviors could complement each other to a certain degree. Essentially, transactional leadership will improve organizational efficiencies; as transformational leadership would steer the organization onto a new course of action and direction tohave a better fit with the changing environment[5]. Although, the external environment of the public organization should determine the appropriate leadership style or mix of leadership styles to adopt, a combination of transactional and transformational leadership has been found most appropriate for United States public organizations[7].

Chapter 11

Transformational leadership: Model for Engineering Changes.

The construct of transformational leadership is used to describe those characteristics of leaders possessing the most effective abilities for navigating turbulent circumstances; and engineering and facilitating requisite organizational changes[20]. The transformational leadership model is, therefore, most suitable for public organizations that require drastic response to changes in the external environments. Such changes may be neccessitated by changes in technology or the need for transistion from old values and behavious to new ones.

Transformational leadership is the model for the organizations under intense external pressure; and need the revolutionary changes necessary for survival[17]. In the strict context, an organization that needs a complete revitalization would require transformational leadership. Transformational leadership is accepted as most appropriate during upheaval or turmoil as in during such crises as organizational failures[1]. When the external environment is dynamic, challenging, and demands quick and correct decisions, transformational leadership could be effective[17]. What is required of the transformational leader is an ability to help the organization develop a vision of what it can be; to mobilize the organization to accept and work toward achieving the new vision; and to institutionalize the changes that must last over time[18].

The three key factors in a transformational model as applied to a public organization are: charismatic leadership, individualized consideration, and intellectual stimulation. Charismatic leadership helps the subordinates appreciate and envision the missions of the organization. Individualized consideration helps focus the leader on the development of the individual subordinate; whereas intellectual stimulation helps to stimulate creativity; so the old problems can be looked at differently, as to enable the development of new ways of finding problem-solving solutions.

As transformational leaders are rare and certainly do not hail from the old school of classical management theory, they are comfortable enacting change; which also means that they are innovative, confident, and willing to take risks in order to achieve the best results for their organizations, citizens, and other stakeholders. Transformational leaders are not only tolerant of followers' mistakes; but also involve them in problem-solving solutions[5]. By remaining open and acceptable to new ideas, they catalyze organizational changes.

This leadership style is quite appropriate for effecting organizational changes because it generates confidence in frightened people and certainty in people who vacillate[4]. This is because transformational leaders strive to create and encourage new learning opportunities for their follower and also tend to acts as mentors[17]. This tendency thus creates optimism where cynicism tends to be prevalent[4]. James Burns had canvassed for transformational leadership; indicating that its popularity hinges on the improvement of the economic performance of subordinates[6]. Individual growth is tied to the organization; and followers are empowered to have a stake in the organization. A transformational leadership, hence, brings about profound and positive changes to public organizations.

By addressing higher level needs, such as esteem, competency, self-fulfillment, and self-actualization; focusing on terminal values such as liberty, equality, and justice; and resting on an ethical foundation; the transformational leader can be a change agent[12]. Generally, they characterize outstanding leadership, which makes them very effective; and they in return produce good results.

As transformational leaders are grounded in the higher level needs of their employees, such as esteem, competency, and self actualization; they are capable of changing entire groups or societies of people, based on their awareness of the needs of their employees and their capacity to assist those employees in meeting their needs[12]. Transformational leaders are, therefore, highly effective as they deal individually with subordinates to meet their developmental needs, and may encourage new approaches and encourage more effort toward developing the solutions to problems[16].

By providing the vision for change[7], the transformational leaders provide change in organizations[8]. To be effective, they must have a clear sense of purpose and goals[8]. A sense of mission and purpose motivates such leaders to recreate and strengthen the organization by enhancing its ability to survive challenging external environments[17]. The ability to emphasize new possibilities while promoting compelling vision for the future makes the transformational leader an effective agent of change[21]. Essentially, the transformational leaders focus on change, progress, and development[21]; thereby creating the mind-set for engineering effective organizational changes.

The desire of the transformational leader toward influencing the way people think and introduce new processes into organization[21], brings it in consonance with the concept of change and leadership as a leaning processes. Moreover, the ability to continuously having fresh looks, trends, and feedbacks from the frontline personnel are two possible catalysts of change[11]. Using internal structures to align and reinforce values and goals, the transformational leader seeks to release human potential into new directions[21]; creating the capacity and potentialities of initiating and managing changes.

Transformational leaders can also act as change agents by motivating their followers to new goals and new behaviors. They hence tend to create action when hesitation exists[4]. Generally speaking, transformational leaders are highly motivational, stressing the achievement of higher collective purpose[2]. As transformational leader appeals to higher needs; they usually strive to change the very nature of an organization or society[12].

Transformational leaders create new organizational pathways[14]. They motivate followers to new and greater good; and thus have the ability to create change[9]. They also focus toward the empowerment of the people for the purposes of building commitment toward organizational goals[22]. These leaders create those energizing characteristics that generate new organizational changes[21]. Thus, they have the capacity to move groups, organizations or societies toward the pursuit of new purposes[10].

Through these efforts at inspiring subordinates by offering and creating challenges; and through individual encouragement for personal development, transformational leaders motivate followers towards commitment to the change process[2]. They, therefore, have the ability to bring a change in attitudes and values of others; which ultimately raise the morals, ethics, and values of a group or the followers.

Transformational leaders also make conscious efforts to increase morality levels in their organizations and among the people who follow them[12]. In an unethical public organization, therefore, a transformational leader could become an agent of change by addressing such higher level needs and terminal values that rest on ethical foundations.

As transformational leadership consists of a set of practices, anyone can function as a transformational leader by adopting these behaviors[12]. In public organizations, this approach holds promise for those wanting to become better and more ethical leaders as transformational leaders are made rather than be born into this role.

A transformational leader is usually an effective facilitator, as his/her method is usually more systematic or perhaps strategic in nature. In other words, a transformational leader looks at the big picture; and focuses on breaking down the strategic steps in a manner that will ensure clear vision and completion of the task at hand. In evaluating a transformational leader, it would be discernable that his or her methods are systematic and process-oriented; as the foundation is usually based on making a vision a reality; with the primary tools being the process and systematic thinking[15].

As the life cycle of an organization also plays a part in the determination of the leadership style to adopt[3], this kind of leadership is most appropriate for managing the new visions, goals, and behaviors that are necessitated by the organizational changes in public organizations; especially, those in need of restructuring and re-orientation. If a public organization is failing, a transformational leader can be effective in revitalizing it. The leader can, however, only be successful if the organizational hierarchy supports his or her mission of change. If there is too much bureaucracy and resistance, and no buy-in from higher authorities, the transformational leader may not be able to realize the new vision.

This leadership model has also been found to work well in such public institutions as the United States military; where, in military operations, there are missions to accomplish; and everyone must do his or her part. A study by the United States Army found that leader behaviour significantly impacts followers extra effort, motivation, and organizational commitment; and that the transformational leadership style is the style most successful in fostering these traits in US Army members[13]. This study strongly shows the appropriateness of interests in transformational leadership behavior and in similar forms of leadership behavior by the military or by other organizations for the development of subordinates and groups as being important for success[13].

Chapter 12

Servant Leadership: Model for Selfless Service

Servant leadership appeals especially to the philosophy of nonprofit organizations, trusteeships, civil right movements, educational systems, community leadership organizations, and training programs related to personal and spiritual growth; and can therefore, be so applied[9]. The servant leadership concept has more to do with serving the needs of the followers or subordinates. The subordinates needs come first and foremost for a servant leader. The motive for actions of a servant leader is characterized by four central concepts, namely; stewardship, obligation, partnership, and elevating purpose. This stewardship would mean that the servant leader acts on behalf of others; protecting and nurturing followers or subordinates. The motivations of servant leaders are derived by this desire to serve. For this, servant leadership is an understanding and practice of leadership that places the good of those led over the self-interest of the leader[6].

A servant leader takes the obligation of working for good of the led ahead of self-interest very seriously. The servant leader therefore, focuses on people; with the primary emphasis on service, rather than on organizational results[10]. Servant leadership is obviously an invitation by Robert Greenleaf to embrace a leadership that is hinged on the state of "the being," rather than "doing"[1].

Servant leaders view their followers or subordinates as partners, and not as subordinates[5]. By sharing leadership in partnership, servant leaders tend to function as "trustees" who do not claim to be better than the people they lead[11]. For elevating purpose, the servant leader serves worthy missions; and seeks to fulfill a higher moral purpose. From this perspective, servant leadership promotes the valuing and development of people, the building of community, and the practice of authenticity[6].

In essence, the servant leadership paradigm views the leader as a servant of the followers; placing the interest of the followers above the self-interest of the leader, emphasizing the personal development and empowerment of the followers[8]. Servant leaders also view leadership from the perspective of opportunity to serve rather than status or position[8]. These are the basic issues that distinguish servant leadership from other leadership models.

When leading in public organizations, servant leaders are characterized by the desire to serve and empower followers; believing that the best way to achieve the set goals would be through the development of the potential of the employees[12]. As the servant leadership model tends to approach leadership from the perspective of leadership development, it allows followers to assume leadership roles when conditions warrant[5].

Taking cognizance of the fact that the servant leadership is focused on the personal growth of the followers, the success of the leader should be measured in terms of extent to which those followers approach self-actualization[7]. Moreover, as servant leadership entails that the leader does not pursue his or her own self-interest; but rather, is primarily concerned with serving others, a servant leader should also be judged by the progress made by his or her followers or colleagues[2].

As this model of leadership emphasizes the leader's role as steward of the resources provided by the organization, it encourages the leader to serve others; while staying focused on achieving results in line with the organization's values and integrity[5]. In addition, they are charged with protecting and nurturing their groups and organizations; while making sure that the collective goals serve the common good[5]. They are also passionate about creating and maintaining an impermeable culture of trust, consistency, and reliability within their organizations. They are empathetic, self-assured and patient. In addition, they realize the importance of recognizing the needs of employees in the context of operational success of the organization. If employees are happy in their work life, there is an excellent possibility that the organization itself will thrive. The practice of servant leadership also requires that decision-making involve most members of the organization, which usually result to consensus[8].

In environments that are low in dynamism, the servant leader's motivation of "service first" is quite effective[8]. The generative and spiritual culture of servant leadership fosters harmony, collaboration, and cooperation; thereby creating the spiritual awareness that is reflective of its core competences. Its emphasis on collaboration and integrity; coupled with communication and persuasion skills, makes servant leadership an effective change agent in such low dynamism environments as nonprofit and the voluntary organizations.

This kind of leadership thrives most effectively in environments or circumstances in which the followers are enlightened; and can hence, develop their collective visions themselves. An example is the legislative assembly (like the Congress) in which the speakers and majority leaders are simply "first among equals"; and can hence become effective as servant leaders. The servant leader in this relationship is precisely the servant and the followers are the masters. A servant leader understands the needs of the master (that is, the followers) because they hear, see, and know the relevant issues; and also have intuitive insight of the proccesses, goals, and objectives of thesubordinates[3].

As the servant leadership model is one in which the leader views himself as a servant to those he leads, the servant-leader is focused on developing a relationship with his followers or subordinates. This is unlike the typical manager in a bureaucratic organization. For some public organizations, this leadership style might raise some concerns about legitimacy since the theory of management is to keep the leader and followers on separate platforms; more segregation than congregation. In bureaucratic public organizations, it can, also be viewed as threatening; particularly, to hierarchical relationships[4].

For public organizations, the servant leadership model can most appropriately be applied to non-profit organizations, trusteeships, education, and community leadership organizations[8]. Obviously, such organizations usually operate in more static environments;

characterized by low and slow changes[8]. That the servant leadership works better in more stable situations or environments makes it most suitable for evolutionary developmental purposes[8]. Unlike transformational leadsrhip, the servant leader is, therefore, more of an evolutionary process than a revolutionary change agent. Hence, servant leaderships are more appropriate in organizational circumstances in which evolutionary changes are desired.

Obviously, this leadership model does not work in every context as the servant leader may be perceived as weak or passive in circumstances where the perception of strong leadership is required. For public organizations, tranformational and servant leadership models are often times compared as both styles demonstrate genuine concerns for their followers. The major reason that transformational leadership attracts more attention is that; in addition to demonstrating concern for their followers or subordinates, they extend their efforts toward applying their skills and talents to engage, motivate, and encourage employees to adapt to specific goals and objectives of the public organization in a manner that ensures quality improvement for not just the organization, but for the employees as well.

PATH IV

POWER & POLITICS in PUBLIC ORGANIZATIONS

Chapter 13

Sources and Constructs of Power in Public Organizations

Power is the potential ability to influence the behavior of others. Power is not the act of changing the behaviour of others, but rather the potential to do so[3]. The basic pre-requisite of power is that a person or group believes it is dependent on another person or group for something of value[3]. Leaders often use their powers to affect the behavior of subordinates. The ability of a leadership to influence people to direct their efforts towards the achievement of some particular goal or goals are derivable from the power such a leader exercises. In a public organization, power represents the resources with which a leader effects changes in the behavior of employees. Sometimes, however, people possess the powers they do not use; or even might not know they have such powers[2].

Power is a two-way traffic between the individual that exercises power and the individuals or groups over whom power is exercised. Essentially, the parties in the power-exchange are interdependent; it is just that a party is more dependent than the other. Although, this one party may be more dependent than the other, a relationship exists only when each party has something of value to offer to the other[3]. The reactions of the subordinates to power, however, vary. The reaction could be in form of commitment to the leader's point of view and instructions, or opposition to such.

Kinds and Sources of Power

The different kinds of power in a public organization are; legitimate power, reward power, coercive power, referent power, and expert power. These power types draw their influences from different sources.

Legitimate power

Legitimate power derives from the values and beliefs by people that someone has the right to exert influence over them; and that as a matter of obligation, they have to comply[1]. Legitimate power comes from formal management position and granted authority; which usually draws compliance. This power comes from the values of others, in which they believe that the power wielder has the legitimate right to influence them. People feel obliged to accept this power; which depends on the wielder's position, rather than on his or her relationship with the power recipient.

Invariably, there is the understanding among members of the organization that people in certain roles can request certain behaviour from others[3]. People who wield legitimate power are obeyed because of their position, and not because of their personalities. More often, when they lose their positions, they lose their powers.

In public organizations, this form of power usually arises from position or titles; as most organizations use them to designate levels of authority. Employees are then influenced by the positions or titles that those people hold in the organizations. It follows therefore, that all employees do have legitimate powers based on their job descriptions, positions, or titles. The filling clerk has the powers to request for somes files based on the job description given to him or her by the organization. A frontline police officer who is called upon to apprehend a criminal or curb gang activities is exercising legitimate power. Similarly, a social worker who has to decide when to unite troubled families or assist victims of child or domestic abuse is exercising legitimate power.

As power can be a two-way authority, a leader's legitimate power rest on, not only on the authority to make discretionary decision, but also on the acceptance of this discretion by followers[3]. All given, this form of command leadership is very prevalent in public organizations.

From a cultural dimension; in such high power distance societies as China, France, India, Turkey, Thailand, Saudi Arabia, Nigeria,

Venezuela, Malaysia, Mexico, and the Philippines, in which individuals accept and support large imbalances in power, status, and wealth; and much respect is shown for those in authority, titles, ranks, and status; employees are more likely to comply with legitimate power. These high power distance societies are those in which individuals accept, and are comfortable, with high inequality in power distribution[2].

Reward Power

Reward power derives from the ability to reward behaviors and performances. This power source draws compliance from the leader's authority to reward. In a public organization, the reward power is derived from a person's ability to control the allocation of the rewards others find valuable; as well as the ability to remove negative sanctions[3]. Transactional leaders usually exercise this kind of power.

As reward power depends on the wielder's ability and resources to reward, the power-recipient must place value on the potential reward. Organizational leaders have reward power in their abilities to grant such rewards as pay raise, promotions, time-offs, favourable vacation schedules, favourable work assignments, praises, and recognitions. If however, the potential recipient does not value these rewards, then the leader does not actually have any reward powers over the employee.

There exists interdependence between the parties; with the individuals over whom reward power is exercised having a counter-power. For instance, a manager may exercise control due to his or her reward power to retain and promote a subordinate. The subordinate does, however, exercise a measure of control through the counter-power that arises from his or her ability to work more productively or less; which in turn would have a positive or negative effect on the manager's job performance evaluation.

In this usual two-way power relationship, employees in public organizations that practice the 360-degree feedback system equally have some counter-powers by virtue of their ability to influence supervisors' promotions and other rewards through their performance or non-performance. It is this counter-power that somewhat compels managers to use their power judiciously, in order to avoid upseting this relationship[3].

An effective leader could use reward power to highlight good works or reinforce behaviours that reflect organizational values[1]. When appropriately used, reward power can help the organization attain its objectives. For instance, reward power could enable the Chief Operating Officer to use performance-based rewards as motivational factors. The reward power, together with legitimate power is common in public organizations and some private organizations.

Coercive Power

The use of coercive power is the leader's authority to punish or withdraw privileges. Coercive power is the opposite of reward power; and is based on the power to apply sactions[1]. Coercive power is the ability to force someone to do something against his or her wish with the main purpose of compliance. Although perceived negatively, governments for instance, use corcive power to maintain law and order in the society. This power source is always dependent on the fear of punishments or ability to withdraw privileges or support. In public organizations, it comes from the expectation that one would be punished or denied privileges if one does not comply with rules, directives, or policies of the organization. The coercive powers that can be used by the leadership in public organizations include; giving poor performance evaluations, initiating transfers, or blocking pay raises.

When an employee performs poorly or behaves unethically, the negative consequences that arise from the applications of coercive power are most appropriate. Such powers should always reside with line managers. Sometimes, subordinates or employees react against coercive power by deliberately avoiding carrying out instructions. In reaction to unfulfilled demands or as tools to pressure management, local labor unions sometimes use coecive power to force their colleagues to working less delligently.

Referent Power

Identifying with others, or having positive regard and respect for others, is a potential source of referent power[1]. Referent power comes from identifying with someone we respect and admire[1]. People, therefore, possess referent powers when others like, identify, or respect them. Essentially, referent power comes from leader's personality characteristics; which not only command subordinate's respect and admiration, but also draw their commitment. As this referent power can also come from a team's identification with their leader's personal characteristics and charisma, this kind of power usualy characterize charismatic leaders. The strenght of this power is, however, dependent on the degree to which others desire to identify with the leader[1].

Generally, the use of reward power tends to increase referent power; whereas the use of coercive power has the opposite effect. As this form of power usually develops from individual interpersonal skills; in public organizations, it sometimes creates situations in which powers and influence over the work teams reside with their functional heads.

Expert Power

Expert power is dependent on the experience and expertise an individual has in an organization; and based on the opinion of others[1]. This power format dwells on the individual's ability to influence others based; on the possessed knowledge or skills that the others deem valuable. When a person has strong knowledge and skills that someone requires, then the individual has expert power. The power also draws from the possession of special expertise, which is needed in an organization. This could include such skills as computer skills, insight into the legislative process, or personal connection with influential persons[1]. The credibility of this power source usually comes from the display of tangible evidence of knowledge.

Like referent power, this form of power originates from within the individual. The hallmark of expert power is that, when a leader is an expert, subordinates go along with instructions because of the leader's supposed superior knowledge. Expert power can also be employee-oriented; leading to empowerment as the "employee knowledge" becomes the means of production; and is ultimately outside the control of those who lead the organization[3].

Chapter 14

Uses of Power and Authority in Public Organizations

Power in public organizations can be described as an exchange between individuals in which one of the individual exerts more control over the outcomes than do the others[2]. Conversely, the concept of authority in organizations is the formal and legitimate right of a manager to make decisions, issue orders, and allocate resources to achieve the goals and objectives of the organization[1]. Leaders of public organizations draw authority from the duties and functions, specified in the legislations establishing the organizations.

Authority occurs where an individual or group complies with a request or orders because of the requester's legitimate power, as well as the individual's role expectation[4]. Authority can hence be viewed as the exercise of legitimized power; or as when power is legitimated, it becomes authority[5]. The differentiating characteristic of authority is that, unlike power, it is vested in positions and not in people. Essentially, whereas authority is vested in a position, power is a personal quality or trait. Moreover, power is associated with leadership, whereas authority is associated with managership. In addition, authority flows vertically down the hierarchy.

Whereas power is the ability to make other people do something; authority is the right to ask other people to do something. Generally, employees in public organizations will comply with managerial authority as a duty, and as defined by the specified legitimate boundaries. A leader may not have the legal right to demand compliance, but may exert influence on others, based on his or her power source, or by creating dependency relationships.

A leader may have the authority to demand high performance from subordinates, but lack the ability to get it done if he or she lacks the power to influence or force them to work harder. Although, an informal leader may not have the formal authority to demand high performance; but can have some power to influence others to perform better.

The influence of authority can be applied through role modeling; assertive application of legitimate and coercive power; or the promise of benefits and rewards for complying with request or orders. Appealing to higher authorities or persuasions are also ways of influencing others in an organization. Sometimes, in public organizations, managers would lack sufficient power form coalition with other managers to be able to influence others. To be highly effective, the leader must combine authority with power.

Uses of Power

Although, the positive use of power is healthy for the organization, the use of power, sometimes, exhibits its darksides as some organizational leaders use such powers for self-serving purposes. For instance, power can be used in a manner that adversely affects the dignity and self-respect of others. Such abuse of power could be destructive to the individuals and the organizations as it interferes with the job performance of the abused. Another instance of destructive use of power is where the leadership manipulates information to influence decision-making; or to serve personal interests. Manipulating such information decreases the quality of the resulting decisions; as well as the outcomes of such decisions.

When exercised, power could either be geared toward upliftment, or toward domination. As the reactions of the subordinates to power vary; the outcome could be compliance or resistance; or could be in form of commitment to the leader's point of view and instructions; or opposition to such. Reward, coercive, and negative legitimate powers tend to produce compliance, and sometimes resistance; while expert, referent and positive legitimate power foster commitment[3]. Of course, commitment is superior to compliance because it is driven by intrinsic motivation[3].

Constructs of Power

The constructs power can be relational or motivational. The relational construct of power indicates that power is a function of relative dependence and interdependence of the actors[2]. In contrast, motivational construct of power presupposes that power and control are used for motivational purposes[2].

In the motivational construct of power, empowerment is achieved by creating the conditions that increase motivation and the feeling of efficacy[2]. Some organizations reward employees with the mindset that salary raises, promotion, and recognition all reinforce and encourage the continuation of desirable performance. This is the motivational construct of power.

In the relational power construct, workers become empowered by delegation of duties[2]. Delegation of authority is the process of granting decision making authority to lower-level employees[3]. This construct views empowerment as the process that creates and enables conditions that increase motivation and feeing of personal efficacy[2].

The relational power construct also encourages the decentralization of authority. The concept of decentralization describes the extent to which authority and accountability is dispersed to the lower employee levels. In a decentralized structure, the decision-making processes are pushed down the line; enabling the involvement of the lower-level personnel. An organization that nurtures a culture of freedom, autonomy, initiative, and challenge is likely to encourage decentralization.

Delegation of authority makes the job of the manager easier; while at same time giving lower-level employees a "sense of belonging" in the organization. Involving members of staff at every level of the decision-making processes allows such organization to tap into the creativity and energy of the employees. This in turn, creates more positive feeling about work and the organization; creating more job satisfaction and greater commitment to the organization. High involvement organizations practice delegation of power by considering employees as partners in achieving their objectives. The positive outcome of delegation of power is, hence, employee empowerment.

Empowerment is the act of recognizing and releasing into the organization, the power that employees already have by virtue of their knowledge, experience and internal motivation[3]. Like the delegation of authority, empowerment also entails the involvement of members of staff at every level in the decision-making process and the subsequent tapping of the creativity and energy of the employees. As in delegation of duties, it also creates more positive feeling about work and the organization; leading to more job satisfaction, and greater commitment to the organization. The key element of empowerment is pushing decision-making progressively down to lower levels[3]. By empowering employees, the total effective power of the organization increases; as everybody would have more input; contributing more to the organizational goals.

The exercise of power or influence in public organizations should not be seen as contests of strenght. Rather, the power or influence should always be transformed into authority.The distribution of power within the oraganization can be made legitimate through the assignment of responsibility; thereby transforming it into authority. Notably, power or influence, when legitimated, becomes authority[5]. By transforming this power into authority, the exercise of influence is transformed and harnassed toward the desired organizational outcome.

As soon as this power is transformed into authority, it should not be resisted and should be maintained; not only by the ability of the leader to allocate resources or apply sanctions; but also by the presures applied, using the norms and values of the organization. Such organizational norms and values add stability to the organizational processes, as well as making the exercise of authority easier and more effective[5].

In public organizations, power should be viewed as a process, rather than a position. A major way to create power as a process is through the delegation of authority or power. Leadership should always delegate and transfer decision-making responsibilities to subordinate staff. This is very necessary because, it goes to improve workplace efficiencies and employees interactions and empowerment.

Chapter 15

Gaining Power: Structures and plays for Power

Organizations cannot be understood by evaluating only their structural dimensions. Organizations also do have functional dimensions; as well as such political dimensions as power, incentives, and conflicts. As the functional dimensions ensure technical expertise, economic efficiency, and professional quality; the political dimension provides the energy that brings about direction or change to the organization.

Power is necessary for positive organizational functioning, and is vital for ensuring organizational survival[1]. In public organizations the power structure is pyramid-like; hence, the higher you go, the fewer the available positions. Power plays arise in organizations when people compete for power and the few top positions.

The structural determinants for understanding the influence and feeling of power in public organizations include; opportunity, mobility, perceived political power, dependency, resource-garnering influence, rewards for subordinates, and numerical representation[1]. The use of power increases when; the level of interdependence among units is high, resources are scrace, there are disagreements on goals, processes are unclear, or there are uncertainties; especially on the use of new technologies[1]. Obviously, the individual with more power is expected to be more successful in achieving his or her goals than the individual with less power[1]. In moments of uncertainties, for instance, the units or individuals that deal with the critical problems acquire power; as they play critical roles in the success of the organization[1]. Under the uncertain and critical periods, power plays central roles in the selection of the new executives that are best suited to deal with the circumstnces; so as to help in ensuring the survival of the most critical components of the organization[1].

Positive and constructive power helps the organization adapt and interact with its environment[1]. Organizational leaders, who use power in positive manners, enhance organizational commitment; as they are usually more focused on building and supporting the confidence and skills of their subordinates[1]. Developing employees by fostering their parcipation, respecting their legitimate values and interests, building their confidernce, and supporting their confidence and skill; is a constructive use of power[1]. Such leaders also use their influence to obtain needed resources for subordinates; providing them with needed information, and dealing with the other organizational problems that might impede them from achieving organizational or unit goals[1]. The leaders who use power in positive manners delegate authority to subordinates, share information, and promote their involvement in the decision-making processses[1]. Doing so enhances the leader's referent power.

To make effective use of organizational power, the leader must be able to make approproiate and positive use of the specific power strategies and tactics. Organizational leaders must be able to influence their subordinates to achieve greater performance; and their superiors and peers to make the right decisions. Leaders who use power appropriately are most likely to have positive influence on others; and are always able to obtain support for their projects and priorities.

In a public organization, the major difference between the constructive use of power and destructive use of power is whether or not it is used for public goals or personal goals[1]. Power is not used constructively when it is used to serve personal needs and agenda. To avoid negative consequences, leaders must combat the wrong use of power as such creates dysfunctionalism in the organization.

Strategies for Acquiring Power

Exploring all possible sources of Power

A strategy for acquiring power in a public organization is being able to explore all possible sources of power within the structures of the organization. As power is derivable from many sources, anything that makes people more dependent on you or you less dependent on others increases your capacity to influence others; which is called power[1]. The power sources, which could be explored and used, include; expertise, respect for others, doing things for others, giving rewards, and recognition. Even when one is in a position of authority in an organization, to get things done, one still needs power to be able persuade others, engender cooperation, or negotiate[1].

Indispensability and Visibility

Being highly skilled and taking on the resposibilities that are critical to the success or enhanced preformance of your unit is a good power-gaining strategy[1]. When an individual becomes skilled or knowledgeable in matters that are critical to organizational performances or success, colleagues, bosses, and surbordinates tend to listen and defer to such an individual. Developing a reputation as an expert on a subject matter that is critical to the success of the organization is a sustainable strategy for gaining power. This creates a measure of dependency of the other individuals on the person that has the special knowledge or skill. Even with this knowledge or expertise, one must, however, be visible enough as to be recognizeable. This visibility can be created by taking on visible assignments, speaking at meetings, or organizing in-house traininigs, workshops and seminars.

Enhancing your Empowerment

Although, empowerment can be fostered by the conditions prevailing in organizations, an individual can enhance his or her empowerment by taking initiatives and by bearing more responsibilites. When confronted with a difficult problem, even before taking such to your boss, it is always better to take the initiative of clearly and concisely identifying the problem and formulating potential solutions and strategies. By taking the initiative and responsibility of developing alternative solutions and recommending the one you consider best, you enhance your efficacy and sense of competency. The boss is more likely to recognize your problem solving skills; giving you more critical responsibilities that could increase his or her dependency on you.

Tactics for Enhancing Power

As there are various strategies one can use to gain power or balance the powers of others, there are also tactics for enhancing the acquired power. As power is a scarce commodity, these tactics and the arising power must be used ethically, legitimately, and effectively as not to deplete one's 'power capital'. In the book, *Organizational Power Politics: Tactics in Organizational Leadership*[2], Gilbert Fairholm indicates the tactics one could use to enhance one's powers as follows:

(i)   Controlling the meeting agenda: in which the individual places his or her self in a position that enables the control of the issues to be discussed in meetings.

(ii)   Selecting the decision-making criteria: by selecting the criteria that will be used for decision-making, one tends to influence outcomes; even without participating in the decision making.

(iii)   Forming coalitions: building and securing alliances with the individuals who are most likely to support or agree you.

(iv)   Co-optation: in which the individual involves those most likely to oppose him or her in the decision making process. By so doing, the co-opted persons become committed to the outcomes of the process.

(v)   Use of external experts: using reputable and well-known external experts will enable one to buttress and legitimate a taken position. Experts can also be used to shield one's self from the burden and potential fallouts of making controversial decisions.

(vi)   Developing surbordinates: by empowering and increasing the capacity of your immediate surbordinates, your overall power increases.

(vii)   Making deals: by making deals involving securing something-for-something agreements with others, you gain more power.

(viii) Building up obligations: doing favors for others; knowing that such favors will be repaid is another way to enhance your powers. Be skillful at always having a positive balance of favours, so as to be in the position to draw on the balance when needed.

Chapter 16

Powerlessness and Power Equalization

Organizational politics is characterized by power, influence, conflict, bargaining, reconciliation, resolution, consesus, and even powerlessness. To be able to protect one's self from the negative consequences of power, an employee must understand the exercise of power and its politics in a public organization. Power has been described as an exchange in which an individual exerts more control over the outcomes than do the others[1]. This form of power becomes more overt when it involves a relationship in which an individual has control over another because the recipient's dependency; or the power wielder's knowledge, reverence, or authority.

Generally, the higher an individual goes up in the organizational ladder, the more access the individual has to information, personnel, and reources. At this point, the individual becomes more resistant to any changes to the existing organizational structures. It becomes a main pre-occupation of the individuals or groups that control the structures and powers within the organization to maintain the status quo. For an effective leadership, paying attention to the power structure in an organization will enable one identify the dependencies, strenghts, the key actors in the implementation of proposals, and the understanding of the trade-offs necessary for goal attainments.

Powerlessness

Often the individuals who control the status quo tend to resist any quests for representativess or diversity in the organization. Under such circumstances, the groups that feel excluded experience some form of powerlessness; and in reaction, tend to develop some negative behaviors or aparthy to the structures of the organization[1]. Powerlessness in public organizations manifest in different forms, namely; gender, racial, and structural powerlessness.

Gender and Racial Powerlessness

Although, power is necessary and healthy for the functioning of the organization, a feeling of powerlessness by a segment of the oraganization can lead to some measure of dysfunctionalism. When individuals are powerless, they are forced to rely only on heirarchical authority; which does not always yield to cooperation, participation, or persuasion. Men and women in the same organization tend to behave differently; not largely for innate gender differences, but rather because of the structuiral characteristics of their job roles and responsibilities[1]. As women are usually clustered in low-power, dependent, and low-mobility positions, it tends to create a sense of powerlessness within the women in the organization[1]. Even when they are placed in higher positions; their lack of numerical representation at the higher levels, and their subsequent inability to command human and material resources perpetuates the feeling of powerlessness[1]. This feeling of powerlessness always leads to such ineffective management behaviors as refusal to delegate; and lack of concern for goals[1]. This same situation also applies to African-Americans in most public and large private organizations in the United States. To correct this, public organization must make conscious efforts to expand opportunities and mobility to everyone, empower people, and balance numerical representation at the top levels[1].

Structural Powerlessness

The powerlessness and its structural characteristics always result to counter-productive behaviors from those who experience the powerlessness. By changing the structure of opportunities, the feeling of powerlessness can be reduced; and its associated negative behaviors greatly diminished. Power delegation can also create the empowerment that could be used to reduce the feeling of powerlessness. The leadership can also reduce powerlessness by making efforts to increase personal efficacy and motivation through participative management and job enrichment.

The powerless can be encouragaed to empower themselves by involving them in the decision-making process; providing them with opportunities for growth and development; and rewarding their initiatives and acts of responsibility[1]. As these empowerment conditions may not always exist in an organizataion, the individual must take the initiative upon his or her self by adopting the strategies to gain power or at the least, equalize the power. For instance, since dependency in organizations is not one-sided as leaders also depend on subordinates for productivity and cooperation; the employee can increase his or her power by increasing the leader's dependency on him or her.

Equalization of Power

Although, organizational leaders may have enormous powers and authority, employees do have some other approaches to balance or equalize such powers. The individuals with less power can equalize the power over them by being mindful that dependence reduces one's power, whereas independence increases one's power. An employee is likely to be more valuable to the organization if the individual has the power to influence others and is self-reliant; than if the individual is powerless and more dependent[1]. To increase one's power in an organization, individuals would have to; (i) be less dependent, (ii) increase alternative sources for meeting needs so as to reduce dependency on others, or (iii) make other individuals more dependent on them.

Being Less Dependent on Others

Generally, leaders in authority gain power over others because; these others depend on the leader for something of value. By decreasing their needs or demands, individuals can make themselves less dependent on the organization. Decreasing dependence on the organization can, however, have less desirable effects on the organization[1].

Developing Alternative sources for Meeting Needs

By developing alternative sources of getting what they want, individuals can be more independent from the organization. By being less dependent on the organization, the individual increases his or her power. This also, can have less desirable effects on the organization.

Making others more Dependent on you

By increasing other individuals' need for us, they can become more dependent on us. If, as an employee, you acquire a special and crucial expertise that no one else has; your boss becomes more dependent on you, and you less dependent on your boss. This is because; gaining this expertise that is critical to the success of the organization can help the organization to do better in accomplishing its missions, goals, and services to the public[1].

Also, when your work functions are central to the functions of your unit or organization, your bosses become dependent on you for the successful performances of the organization; at least to an extent. Increasing the dependence of others on you, while not decreasing your dependence on the organization, can also increase your involvement in the organization; thereby making you more valuable to the organization[1].

PATH V

THE STRATEGIC OPTIMIZATION of LEADERSHIP in PUBLIC ORGANIZATIONS

Chapter 17

Nature of Public Organizations and their Leaderships

Citizens are usually the focus of any democratic government; and hence, the allegiance of the public organizations is to the public. The appropriate natures of public organizations and the nature of their leaderships have for a long time been subjects of intense debates. The strength of public organizations emanate from the perceptions that its actions are representative of the wishes of the people. Hence, the values that have evolved from the public organizations include; equality of the citizenry, the responsiveness and accountability of the government to the governed, the transparency of government actions and services, and the accessibility of all to government programs and services. For this reason, among others, most elements of public programs carry social undertones.

The structures

The objectives and rationale of conventional concepts of public administration has always been the economical, efficient, and coordinated management of public services[13]. By virtue of their public trust, public managers and leaders must promote values that go beyond efficiency, effectiveness, and economy; and also emphasize responsiveness, equity, and public service[16]. It therefore follows that the analysis of the success or otherwise of public programs must take cognizance of the fact some of these programs are meant to ensure social and economic equity; and in some cases, address inequalities. Social equity is fairness in the delivery of public services; that is, the principle that each citizen regardless of economic resources or personal traits, has the right to equal treatment by the political system[14].

The structures of public organizations tend to be in mechnistic organizational form. Public organiizations, therefore, usually have narrow spans of control and high degrees of formalization and centralization[10]. They have hierarchical structures, use standardized methods, and have clearly defined lines of authority, communication, and decision making[5]. They usually have many rules and procedures, with limited decision-making taking place at the lower levels. Public organizations also usually have tall hierarchies of people in specialized roles[10]. Information and communication flows vertically downwards, and not horizontally. They also have clearly bounded roles, with tasks rigidly defined.

Modern day public organizations, especially those operating in unstable and uncertain territories; such as those in counter-terrorism and emegency services should, however, have the organic structures; with changing lines of authority, informal communication, distributed decision making, and fluid role definition[5]. Under this organic structure, the span of control becomes wider; decision making is decentralized; with the tasks as fluid as being able to adjust to new situations and new organizational needs.

Organizational Cultures

Organizational culture is a system of shared values, assumptions, beliefs, and norms that unite the members of an organization[7]. The formal structure of an organization is a reflection of its organizational culture. When the culture of an organization is consistent with its strategy, the implementation of the strategy becomes a lot easier. Successfully implementing a strategy that contradicts organizational culture is usually difficult.

Sometimes, informal cultures or subcultures may develop in a public organization. These informal cultures can be viewed as the interpersonal relationship in the organization that affect decisions within it; but are omitted from the formal scheme or are not consistent with it.

These subcultures can, at times, act as spawning grounds for emerging values that keep the firm aligned with the needs of customers, employees, society and other stakeholders[10]. Subcultures or informal cultures can, therefore, help replace the dominant values with the values that appropriately reflect the changing environment. Under such perspectives, suppressing the subcultures can create a situation where it takes the organization longer time to align itself with the emerging values and environment.

The informal cultures or subcultures can also develop into counter-cultures, opposing the organization's core values; and can potentially create conflict and dissension among employees. The subcultures are, therefore, also capable of working against the strategic goals and objectives of the organization.

Nature of Leaderships

For reasons of structures and functions, leaderships in public organizations tend to be transactional; with the leader managing rather than leading. The leadership functions in public organizations always involve the bestowal of formal authority on the occupant of a position by a higher organizational authority[14]. The legitimacy of leadership is therefore, derivable from the legal and perceived rights that come with the position. Powers in organizations are usually hierarchical with supervisors or organizational leaders bossing over the surbordinates.

The bureaucratic nature of organizations creates an undue emphasis on legitimate power and respect for rules, procedures, and tradition[11].This bureaucratic mangement mentality that pervades public organizations tends to emphasize caution, compliance, patriarchal leadership styles, and narrow self-interest[3].

Leadership of public organizations usually place value on stability and order; but not of efficiency and better performance. The leadership prefers work processes in ordered settings; guided by regulations, as the leaders seek to change the status quo in evolutionary ways[3]. More often, these leaders tend to exhibit impersonal or even passive attitudes toward goals; probably because they are not usually involved with the set goals[3].

In some public organizations, however, effective leadership can be a catalyst for new strategic management initiatives[1]. The responsible public leadership should not only demonstrate; but should also be adjudged to demonstrate effectiveness, ethics, and endurance[17].

Leaders of public organizations should be more concerned with issues that have meanings to people, and should always endeavour to carry the people along. A challenging issue about the provision of public services is, however, the difficulty of bringing them to measurable parameters. Obviously, such issues as cost of pollution, satisfaction, and social equity are not intangible; but the only problem is the insistence on using the tools for evaluating business processes on the public sector.

Influence of National Cultures

Although, leadership is essential to the functions of organizations within societies; the attributes and the characteristics for leadership vary across cultures[4]. The culture of the organization, which is a by-product of societal culture, affects the individual's values, ethics, attitudes, assumptions, and expectations[9]. A cultural co-relation also exists between the leadership styles of an individual and the acceptance of such styles by subordinates. There is, therefore, a cultural dimension to the kind of leadership that evolves in a public organization within a society.

In considering the influence of culture on leadership and followership, it is necessary to understand Geert Hofstede's studies on national cultures. The Dutch Scholar, Geert Hofstede had analyzed cultural dimensions from the five perspectives of of power distance, individualism versus collectivism, masculinity versus femininity, and uncertainty avoidance[8a]. In simple terms, these respectively mean; the analysis of how people accept social inequality (power distance), the bond between individuals and societal groups (individualism versus collectivism), to what extent people embrace competitive masculine traits or nurturing feminine traits (masculinity versus femininity), and to what extent people strive to control their situations (uncertainty avoidance).

Power distance and uncertainty avoidance are the two dimensions of culture that have most profound influences on leadership in organizations[8a]. Power distance refers to the manner a societies addresses physical, material, and intellectual inequalities within its structure and politic. Some cultural types allow inequalities to grow over time until there is great separation of power and wealth; whereas others attempt to minimize the inequalities by redistributing power and wealth[8a]. The cultural types that allow inequalities to grow are termed large power distance; while those that minimize inequalities are termed small power distance[8a].

In small power distance societies, individuals strive for power equalization and justice. The small power distance Anglo-American, Nordic, and Germanic cultures place more emphasis on competence than on seniority. These cultures minimize inequalities, favor less autocratic leadership, and favor less centralization of authority.

In small power distance societies, subordinates, and superiors perceive and treat each other as likes that have equal rights; and subordinates expect to have inputs in the decisions or actions affecting them[8b]. In these societies, subordinates expect to be consulted when decisions are been made. These tend to create situations in which the leadership styles in such societies are usually participatory.

Small power distance societies are more likely to support and nurture the ethical leadership; as they usually expect and demand that power be legitimate. Public leaderships are therefore, usually acquired and changed through constitutional and legal means. Corruption is less tolerated as scandals usually end careers; and can always lead to legal sanctioning.

Conversely, large power distance societies accept and support large imbalances in power, status, and wealth; much respect is shown for those in authority; and titles, ranks, and status are revered. These cultures have greater acceptance for inequalities and authoritarian leadership. Large power distance societies are common in the Arab, Asian, African, Latin Europe, and Latin American countries. They include such countries as China, France, India, Turkey, Thailand, Saudi Arabia, Nigeria, Venezuela, Malaysia, Mexico, and the Philippines.

Large power distance societies are usually status-conscious; respecting age and seniority; and bestowing outward importance on protocol, formality, and hierarchy. Superiors are expected to lead by making decisions either autocratically or paternalistically; and the subordinates are generally afraid and unwilling to disagree with their superiors[6]. Subordinates, therefore, expect to be told what to do; and they wilfully obey.

The high degree of centralization, which is attributable to the reluctance to delegate functions, which arises from the lack of trusts on subordinates' ability to perform, is a reflection of the large power distance[15]. Also, the autocratic leadership characteristic of public organizations in some countries is indicative of the existance of large power distance[12].

The large power distance societies usually show less concern to whether or not power is legitimate; and therefore, may not always expect nor demand ethical leadership. Corruption could be prevalent and frequent; as scandals are usually covered up, and does not always lead to the end of public careers or to legal sanctions. Public leadership is usually autocratic, and may be changed through unconstittutional means.

Uncertainty avoidance refers to the degree of tolerance or acceptance a society has for surprises, ambiguity, risk, or chance factors[8b]. This dimension also refers to the extent to which people seek orderliness, consistency, structure, and laws[8b]. This dimension also refers to the degree to which individuals in the society feel uncomfortable in risky, uncertain, or unpredictable situations; and the degree to which the society favors conformity or is tolerant of deviant ideas.

Strong uncertainty avoidance societies are common in Latin America, Latin Europe, Japan, and Germanic Europe. The strong uncertainty avoidance societies try to create security and avoid risks by using such instruments as rules and laws; expertise and formal institutions; or religion. In these societies, people feel threatened by uncertainty and show little tolerance for deviation. These strong uncertainty avoidance cultural types attempt to formulate ways of controlling future events, thereby reducing the level of uncertainty and risks[8a].

In weak uncertainty avoidance societies as the Nordic and Anglo countries; and moderate uncertainty avoidance countries as the United States; people, to varying degrees, are reasonably tolerant of uncertainty, ambiguity, different behaviors and opinions. They do not feel threatened by such differences, and are also willing to accept personal risk. These weak uncertainty avoidance cultural types accept higher levels of risk; and therefore, do not attempt to control an uncertainty; but rather socialize members of the society to accept it[8a]. The tendency to accept fate, the tolerance of ambiguity, and the preoccupation with the immediate are indications of weak uncertainty avoidance societies; and can create leadership characteristics that militate against strategic planning; as it requires consideration for the future[8a].

Some scholars believe that the strong uncertainty avoidance cultures may require more transaction-based leadership; whereas weak uncertainty avoidance cultures will tolerate more innovative and transformational behavior[2]. Some other scholars believe that because of the unquestionable respect and obedience to authority inherent in large power distance cultures; transformational leadership is more effective in such cultures[2]. It does, therefore seem that when a society has the weak uncertainty avoidance and large power distance cultural dimension, the appropriate leadership model would be a combination of the leadership competences that suits it cultural orientation.

The lesson of the influence of culture on leadership is that strategic leadership entails the appreciation of any possible diversity that exists in the workplace. Obviously, there are opportunities, as well as challenges that abound in diversified workplaces. Diversified workplaces offer creativity, energy, and new approaches to solving problems. The differences in background can also lead to challenges that could result to conflicts, disruption, and loss of productivity. Organizations and individuals operating in culturally diverse societies must consider how their actions affect such societies; as well as how the corresponding ethical norms in these societies affect the subsequent behavior and decision making process of their organizations and employees. For instance, does the organization consider only the "value of Honesty" in absolute terms or the "value of that honesty" in the context of the cultural and social systems?

Chapter 18

The Leader as the 'Master of Change' and 'Chief Motivator'

Change by definition, requires creating a new system; which in turn always demands leadership[10]. The behaviors of organizational leaders directly influence actions in the ever-changing work environments[7]. Leadership has a role in creating a culture of continual and sustainable changes in these ever-changing environments. The changes in the environment are tell-tale signs for the internal mechanism of the organization to act; preparing employees for upcoming changes[12]. Considering that leaders are responsible for the change strategy, implementation, and monitoring, they function as change agents; as well as motivators.

Leader as the 'Master of Change'

The challenges of managing change are the profound roles of leaders[2]. In effect, leaders that create, support, and implement continuous and transformational changes remain capable of meeting organizational goals[4]. Today's leaders should not only be able to respond to changes and lead their public organizations to survival, but must also transform their structure, functions, methods of service delivery for the effective advancement of organizational missions[1].

The strategic responsibility of leadership is to be tuned and responsive to the ambient environment; to identify and understand the implications of change, to determine the courses of action, and guide their implementations[9]. The chief executive, as the 'master of change', must create a compelling vision to move the organization forward in this era of limits, change, turbulence, and scarcity of resources[9]. The role of the leader in the strategic leadership paradigm is that of the 'master of change'.

Notably, a strong organizational culture could constitute a hindrance to change by preventing the accurate assessment of the external environment[12]. For an enduring change to occur, it must be such that would pervade the entire organizational culture[12]. Some organizations, however, remain static even when the need for changes exist; and transformation only begins when a new leader who appreciates the need and essence of organizational changes emerges[10].

Generally, such a leadership model as the trait-based leadership model by its nature and essence creates perspectives and environments that are resistant to changes[2]. Likewise, the command-and-control styles of management implicit in transactional leadership are inimical to the innovative behaviors that engineer change. Moreover, transactional leaders usually have a sense of commitment to the organization and tend to conform to organizational norms and values, and are therefore not active change agents. On the other hand, transformational leadership has the capacity to move groups, organizations or societies toward the pursuit of higher purposes[6], and by appealing to higher needs, strive to change the very nature of an organization[8]. This kind of leadership is most appropriate for managing the new visions, goals, and behaviors necessitated by the organizational changes. Obviously, the servant and transformational models could be both tied to change perspectives. However, whereas the servant leadership is appropriate for evolutional changes, transformational leadership suits revolutionary changes[14].

Some organizational leadership can, however, create barriers to changes especially when they design strategies that undermine organizational values. Leaders can also be more concerned with protecting their places rather than what is the best interest of the organization. Hence, the leader can bear the contradiction of being an unconscious resistor of change and the guardian of the status quo[12]. In organizational changes, especially when innovative can also consume the leaders; and the leader can, thus become both the enabler and victim of change[12].

Leader as the 'Motivator-in-Chief'

Leadership can also be described as that evolving interrelationship in which leaders continuously receive motivational responses from followers[3]. There are, however, certain characteristics that followers expect from motivational leaders. They want leaders who appreciate them, involve them, and respect their worth as individuals; and who are accessible and who communicate with them for who they are, and not as means to organizational goals[16]. Some followers want recognition for their uniqueness or diversity in race, gender, age, sexual orientation, ethnicity, and marital status[16]. These are similar to those psychological contents of the job motivation as achievement, recognition, responsibility, and advancement that are spelt out in Frederick Herzberg's motivator-hygiene theory. Most of these motivational factors are value-based; and when jobs are aligned to employee values, worker retention is high[16]. Value-based perspective to job alignment must, however, take cognizance of the diversity of the employees[16].

When these leadership characteristics are absent or are lost, most followers, employees, or volunteers lose their motivation. The lessons the Herzberg's motivation theory offers to organizations remain relevant; the provision of the basic physiological needs as supervision; salary; interpersonal relations, status, security, and working conditions can eliminate job dissatisfaction, it would not, however, motivate to high levels of achievements. On the other hand, the presence of the motivators as growth and esteem needs is likely to promote high performance and satisfaction.

Understanding the impact of the various leadership styles on employee motivation and empowerment is necessary for the purpose of identifying the most effective leadership styles for public organizations. Transactional leadership motivates followers by appealing to Maslow's lower order needs of food, shelter, safety, and affiliation[18]. The key element of transactional leadership is contingent rewarding in which leaders motivate by rewarding good performances[15].

The motivations for the followers of transformational leaders, in contrast, rest on the foundation of mentorship, inspiration, individual development, and the achievement of higher collective purpose[18]. The transformational leaders inspire and motivate employees through their charismatic traits and abilities, and by appealing the higher needs. Transformational leaders are usually charismatic and can arouse the consciousness of followers to new outcomes and motivate them to rise above their own interests for common goals[5]. Superior performances are more possible through the stimulation and motivation of followers to higher level of ideal that transformational leadership ushers[11]. This is more easily achieved by transforming the values, attitudes, and motives of followers from lower to higher levels[13]. Transformational leaders hence, motivate by appealing to such Abraham Maslow's higher order needs such as esteem, self-fulfillment, and self-actualization[18].

Collaboration and networking have also assumed more prominence in leadership structures; with regards to motivation. The positive attributes of collaboration and networking are; the capacity to address common problems, share common resources, and create learning environment and opportunities; thereby sharing common goals[17]. The fundamental challenge toward effectively leading and solving any public problem in a collaborative setting is the integration of knowledge among stakeholders and participants[17]. This knowledge of integration is necessary as collaboration in leadership could also serve as a tool for motivation.

The role of the organizational leader as the "chief motivator" is, therefore, to strive to remove the 'dissatisfiers' by providing the basic needs; and then use the motivators to propel workers toward greater achievement and job satisfaction. Also, it is necessary that the leader becomes a collaborative capacity-builder; developing the appropriate mind-set and guides; as he or she integrates the common knowledge toward building the required problem-solving capacity[17].

Chapter 19

Leadership Strategies during Organizational Changes

Organizational changes portend much uncertainty; and as such, the challenges of making changes remain profound in the roles of leadership[8]. These changes are usually needed when an organization needs to make a change from one type of culture to another, or to incorporate another culture type[3]. For instance, making a transition from entitlement culture for which public organizations are noted to a more responsive revitalization culture will require leadership. Even the sustainability of positive changes implies that new working methods and performance levels be created through leadership[1]. There is, therefore, the need to understand organizational changes with respects to its phases and the roles of leadership.

The continuous changes that affect private organizations also affect public organizations. Like private organizations, public organizations are also constantly in need of improvement in order to remain responsive to the needs and demands of their customers (citizens). In both situations, whereas resources are shrinking, the demands for accountability and competition for the scarce resources are increasing.

Generally, organizational leaders influence the actions in the work environment[8]. Leaders are, however, not only expected to react to changes; but also, to be agents of change when necessary[20]. The most effective strategies for leading change is by motivating and communicating effectively with the employees; as well as creating the environments in which the change champions can thrive[8].

In dealing with the various constructs of public organizations and organizational changes, there is need to address the various issues that are relevant to organizational changes; especially, with respect to the stakeholders and the external change drivers that strive to influence changes in the organizations. Obviously, the manner these transformations take place in relation to leadership and stakeholders' relationship; and to the global and societal interests, demand a good measure of consideration. The evaluation of the ability of organization to enable change is, hence, important from both the perspectives of facilitation and that of accountability to the stakeholders.

Notably, leaders who effectively implement the change processes usually possess such skills as the abilities to motivate, communicate, build teams, mentor and coach, involve others, and appropriately reward performance[8]. By serving as role models for instance, such leadership styles as transformational leadership behaviours correlate to performances[7].

Leadership in Challenging Times

Leading a public organization during periods of turmoil; or during the internally or externally induced organizational changes involves strategic leadership, human resources, management, and planning. Leaders who run public organizations during environmentally or self-induced changes must, therefore, embrace certain strategic practices. Such practices include the delegation of authority, devolution of power, talent identification employee participation, overcoming resistances, and motivating the unwilling.

Generally, leaders play crucial roles in preparing for the change; especially, during the change process, and after the implementation of the change programmes[21]. Obviously, employees will look towards the leaders for effective planning, effective decision making, and complete communication. Moreover, employees become committed and motivated when they perceive leadership as supportive, concerned, and committed to their welfare[21]. It is therefore necessary that leaders create a trust environment throughout the entire periods of change.

The strategic processes to adopt during the challenging organizational changes include: scanning the environment, talent identification, encouraging the adoption of the appropriate change culture, delegation of power, decentralization of authority, provision of resources, setting performance goals and rewards, overcoming resistances, motivating the unwilling, discouraging 'group thinking', and developing feedback mechanisms.

In analyzing this role of leadership in creating a culture of continual and sustainable changes in this ever-changing environment of public organizations, it is, however, worthy to note that adaptive changes are usually less threatening than innovative changes.

Scanning the Environmental for Changes

The external environments that drive changes can be technological, economic, legal political, social, or cultural; hence, environmental scanning should be non-negotiable to the leader of any public organization[14]. These changes in the environment are telltale signs for the internal mechanism of the organization to act. Environment scanning involves the collation of the relevant data; and analysis of such data as they affect the organization. Usually, environmental scanning results to the understanding of the effects of change in organization; assisting forecasting and relating change expectations to decision-making.

An effective environmental scanning programme enables the decision maker to understand current and potential changes taking place in the external environments[7]. As the environments of organizations affect their ability to successfully carry out their public roles and duties; public organizations need to understand their future environments within the context of their goals, objectives and strategies[9]. As there are constant needs for effective and continous scanning of the external environment; organizational leaders should always prepare employees for any upcoming changes.

The response behavioral profile for the scanning includes: stability, reactiveness, anticipation, exploration, and creativity; all of which should be deployed as effective responses to environmental changes. The strategic responsibility of the organizational leader remains being tuned and responsive to the ambient environment; identifying and understanding the implications of change; as well as determining courses of actions; and guiding their implementation[12].

Talent identification (Identifying Team leaders)

There are numerous ways through which leaders could recognize the unique talents and contributions of subordinates or employees; and their subsequent identification as high potential employees. Typically, a person's perceived attitude, willingness, and ability to excel as a leader; interpersonal, and communication skills; and personal performance as rated on a performance matrix, are key factors in leadership identification. Critical thinking skills are also talents that leaders readily recognize. The originality of thinking, specialized skills, fresh perspective to issues, and good problem-solving skills are also some of the critical skills recognizable to an effective leader[2].

These high potential employees will progress to leadership roles by acting as mentors or team leaders; in which case, the individual is empowered with the responsibility to train teammates and also act as the leaders of the teams. The ability of a team leader to manage a change process will entail innovativeness; and the ability to communicate new vision and strategic plans to colleagues; as well as management skills. The management then supports such high talent employees by helping them build up the capabilities they need for meeting the new challenges.

Encouraging the appropriate change culture

Obviously, the prevailing organizational culture may not support the change processes. The way employees work, their attitudes toward work and change, their relationships with each other and management; always have effects on the change process[21]. Sometimes, the prevailing organizational culture can constitute a roadblock to successful implementation of structural change programs by making meaningful initiatives vulnerable to cultural influences[9a]. Encourgaing the appropriate change culture is, therefore, an important part of the change management process.

Decentralization of Authority

As the decentralization of authority describes the extent to which authority and accountability are extended to the lower employee levels; and decision-making pushed down to the lower levels, the concept is relevant to strategic leadership. Especially, as involving more members of staff at every level in the decision-making unleashes the creativity and energy of the employees; helping to create more positive feeling and greater employee commitment.

Moreover, the self-organizing principles of modern management do no longer require the command-structured top-down management style[19]. Such command styles should be discarded because even public organizations are becoming complex systems, and such not very predictable; especially, in terms of the problems they have to confront and solve. In some public organizations, as the problems that confront leaderships are increasingly becoming less predictable. Due to such unpredictability, even small changes can have massive and unanticipated effects.

The organizational structures of most public entities have, however, remained hierarchical; with powers concentrated at the top level. Little wonder higher levels of job dissatisfaction exist in the public sector than either the private or nonprofit sectors.

Delegation of Power

Effective leadership in public organizations is usually accomplished through dedication, hardwork, and cooperation from the people[4]. Effective leaders are more likely to delegate their powers to subordinates, reward their subordinates; as well as provide teamworks that enhance the powers of their subordinates. When a leader shares powers with subordinates, the overall power of each party increases as the subordinates, in return, give the leader more referent power. As both parties increase the amount of influence they exert over each other, the result is the net increase in their individual powers.

As modern leadership principles have become people-oriented, a public organization optimizes its leadership capacities by delegating and transferring decision making responsibilities to subordinate staff. As delegation is the process granting decision-making authority to lower-level employees[13]; high involvement leadership organizations practice this concept by considering employees as partners in the achievement of organizational objectives. The concept of delegation empowers employees by extending the processes to lower-levels, producing the positive outcome of interweaving power and authority. Notably, leadership becomes highly effective, when power and authority are combined.

The delegation of power makes the job of the leadership easier; and at the same time enthrones higher job satisfaction levels among the subordinates. Obviously, an individual will believe that the goals of a group are important, if he or she has been part of establishing those goals[3]. Public organizations become more responsive by delegating and transferring decision-making responsibilities to subordinate staff. This form of empowerment will create better participation and creativity.

In addtion, the transfer of decision-making responsibilities to subordinate staff also improves workplace efficiencies and employee interaction. Moreover, as public organizations are supposed to view power as a process rather than a position; a method for achieving this is largely through the delegation of power.

Provision of Resources

In the constructive use of power, leaders support the confidence and skill of the employees by providing them with the resources required for their effective performances during the change process. These leaders will obtain the needed resources for their subordinates; providing them with the information and material resources they need for achieving organizational or unit goals.

For project teams, the total manpower and resource needs of each team are worked out; enabling each team to know what is needed from the perspective of both manpower and resources. This should also include offering additional resources to overcome any lack of skills. Employees will appreciate such assistance as offering additional resources, identifying crucial competences, training, and addressing employees' concern. It is imperative that such needs should fall within the resourses and capabilities of the organization. Obviously, employees cannot be expected to assume new and unfamiliar responsibilities and authorities without support from their leaders[10]. By providing them with these necessary resources for undertaking the change process, the entire process is facilitated.

Setting Performance Goals and Rewards

To make the change and transformational processes successful, the leaders should seek ways to obtain clear performance improvements by establishing goals and planning systems that are designed to achieve objectives; as well as rewarding the high achievers[11]. Using rewards to reinforce new behaviors and accomplishment can be motivating. Motivation by rewards, may, however, not be applicable to every employee as cultures and values tend to play some roles too.

Obvioulsy, certain leadership and management principles tend to have universal appreciation; and, no matter the cultural orientation, the practices of goal setting, performance feedback, and valued rewards will improve the performances of employees[16]. Setting new standards for performance evaluation, and creating metric sheets and progress reports to reflect progress will be effective strategies.

Overcoming Resistances

People resist changes for a variety reasons that include; fear of the unknown, self-interest, job security, and the apprehension about new structures or new ways of doing things. Even the introduction of new yardsticks for performance evaluation can cause some measure of apprehension. For the unit leaders, threats to power and influence, and the pontentialities of administrative or technological changes that could alter the bases and balances of power or threaten jobs, can also bring about resistance.

Building momentum by highlighting short-term wins; developing coalition, and marshalling the efforts of employees toward common visions can help leaders overcome the possible resistances[11]. The usual way forward is to identify the employees' needs, fears, and potentials; and to allay those fears and harness the potentials.

Motivating the Unwilling

There are two cogent ways for influencing the unwilling, unconcerned, or unmotivated. These could either come from the exercise of raw power, or through leadership. Power remains the potential ability to influence the behavior of subordinates irrespective of the means used to achieve the purpose. Conversely, leadership influences subordinates to direct their efforts toward the achievement of some particular goal or performance. Leadership would usually motivate subordinates to realize and use their latent potentials.

As the ability of a person in authority to influence and motivate subordinates to direct their efforts toward the achievement of some particular goals are derivable from the power such a leader exercises;

the outcome could either be compliance, or resistance.

Influencing the unwilling, unconcerned, or unmotivated requires the acknowledgement their points of view; and not demonizing their perspective[18]. Demonizing the perspective of others leads to loss of mutual respect. Developing processes that portray mutual respect and collaboration leverages the ability of the leader to motivate his or her subordinates. In essence, influencing subordinates demands that they be made to realize their own capabilities; and then influencing them to use such capabilities. When, essentially, it is put to good use, power could focus on either uplifting the individual; whereas when misused it focuses on dominating the individual.

Discouraging 'Group Thinking'

Generally, maintaining the polarities of opinion could generate and enhance organization development by encouraging creativity and innovativeness. On the surface, polarities of opinion tend to lead to the creation of sub-cultures. As these subcultures are usually the harbingers of polarities of opinions, they could become the spawning grounds for the emerging values that keep the organization constantly aligned with the needs of citizen-customers, employees, and other stakeholders[15]. By helping to replace the dominant values with values that appropriately reflect the changing environment, sub-cultures encourage polarity of opinions; and hence, could be catalyst of transformational changes.

In reality, however, this is not often the case because of issues of "group thinking". "Group thinking" is a situation where group members are culturally pressurized to agree with mainstream thinking for fear of been characterized as saboteurs or as ignoramuses; or to please the group or those in power or authority. "Group thinking", as the consensus thinking within a group, interferes with the ability to make informed decisions as group members have suppressed criticisms about a proposed course of actions[17]. When an organization suffers from "group thinking", creativity is dampened and the flow of information stifled. This is because, the tendency in a 'group thinking' situation is to play down the minority opinion, and even suppress such through the application of pressure on members who disagree or entertain doubts on the chosen line of action. This is usually a prevalent situation in most public organizations.

Creating a feedback Mechanism

Using the information garnered during the stages of the change processes can provide the feedbacks that are required for the development of effective leadership strategies. Managing any resistances will also mean using any information provided as feedbacks to realign relationships in the course of achieving the desired goals[5]. This entails using the information so provided to design the processes that are required to build commitments to the change processes. The feedback mechanism can also be obtained through "integrative resistance"; whereby the pieces of information from the resistance feedbacks are used to design improvements for the processes.

Chapter 20

Strategies for Optimizing Leadership

As leadership in a public organization is describable as a system of interacting inputs that create and deliver purpose within the performance system and environment within which leadership occurs; it does mean that such a leadership does not exist in a vacuum[21]. Rather, it is the nature of followership and the performance system that shape the leadership of a public organization[14]. Every performance system has a constituency that represents those whom the leadership not only serves, but for whom it also produces the desired results[14]. The stakeholders and the constituencies that the leadership serves define the goals of the performance systems.

As organizational leadership is also the process of influencing people to direct their efforts towards the achievement of some particular goal or goals[8]; leadership qualities should include the ability to identify the various concerns of the followers and the social network at the workplace. Moreover, as leadership, unlike naked power wielding, is inseparable from followers' needs and goals; effective leadership must address the needs and aspirations of the employees[17].

Leadership skills should not only include this ability to identify the various concerns of followers; but should also include the knack for seeking the opportunities hidden in every problem. Leaders, who are focused on the issues of concern to people, always endeavour to carry the people along. Although, the behaviour and language of leadership are very necessary ingredients for effective leadership; often, the legitimacy of leadership is derivable from personal attributes that are anchored on a charismatic disposition. For utmost effectiveness, leaders should always: (i) understand their roles, (ii) define the significant stakeholders to interact with, (iii) build the teams, and (iv) implement the plan with the people and (v) create cross-functional teams to solve the identified problems[6].

Optimizing Leadership Potentials

The phenomenon of leadership in a public organization comes with the need to achieve the goals desired by the internal and external stakeholders of a specific performance system[21]. For public organizations, these stakeholders are the tax paying members of the system, the citizens, the legislating bodies, and the policy makers. Public organizations must, therefore, develop and implement strategies that would help them develop and nurture the leadership that would not only meet organizational goals; but also create long-term values that would conform to the values of the stakeholders. In essence, leadership at all the levels in a public organization must be based on the respect for the dignity and self-worth of others, commitment to organizational goals, and adherence to the ethics of public service[5].

For its maximum value optimization, public organizations need leaderships that can create and follow through with their missions and visions. The visions need to be clear, compelling and energizing; serving as a unifying focal point of efforts. Vision, in essence, is the substance of good leadership. If a vision is the substance of a transforming leadership, then communicating that vision is the process[16]. This is actualizable through the creation and implementation of communication strategies that consistently communicate the new vision and strategic plans to employees and other stakeholders. This, however, requires thinking beyond current capabilities and environment.

Public organizations also need leaderships that involve employees in the decision-making processes. Effective leaders build the commitment of the employees by involving them in the process of shaping the the visions of the organization[16]. By empowering employees, the total effective power of the organization increases; as employees would be more involved in contributing to the organizational goals.

The strategies for optimizing leadership potentials in public organizations include; communicating the organizational vision and missions, empowering the employee, developing the skills of the employees, treating the organization as a learning organization, developing feedback mechanisms, and providing ethical leadership.

Communicating the Vision and the Mission

For its optimization, public leadership requires communicating the visions, goals, roles, and responsibilities; inspiring confidence in leadership direction and resources, resolving issues, and delivering results[13]. This is necessary as any leadership that conceptualizes the future, will align goals with the common vision; as well as provide the inspirations needed to achieve transformational goals[11]. For a public organization to be effective in accomplishing its public purposes, the employees must not only understand the organizational values and goals, they must internalize them[5].

The implementation of strategies that consistently communicate the new visions and strategic plans to employees would assist a public organization in actualizing them. This is because a vision that is held only by an organization's leadership is not enough to create real and sustainable changes[12]. In this, the functional heads would have to be the arrowheads of the communication processes.

Leaderships in public organizations should also be accessible to employees, with enough face-to-face forums for addressing employee issues; as well as sharing the articulated vision of the new strategic orientation. Effective interpersonal communication, which is the ability to understand and be sensitive to the feelings, thoughts, and situation of other people, is of utmost importance to effective leadership. In organizational leadership, leaving out the key element of interpersonal communication could constitute a barrier to high involvement leadership. The laid out procedures for ensuring accessibility could also serve as an effective feedback system.

Employee empowerment through high involvement Leadership

As high-involvement leadership creates a clear, compelling, and energizing vision that serves as a unifying focal point of efforts, high involvement organizations view employees as partners in achieving their objectives. By providing opportunities for employee involvement in decision making, showing respect, giving trust and ehnacing their growth potentials, employees become more empowered[5]. These create more positive feeling about work and the organization; especially on job satisfaction and commitment to the organization.

High involvement leadership also entails guidance and support from the leadership to employees; as employees cannot be expected to assume new and unfamiliar responsibilities and authorities without much guidance and support from their leaders[9]. In public organizations, however, there could be such barriers to leadership involvement in employee empowerment that may include: the under-investment of money and time, the lack of appropriate rewards for high-involvement practices, mistrust for leaders, and the lack of self-motivation among frontline employees[9]. Mistrust is a crucial issue that inhibits teamwork; and a sure way to overcome this mistrust is to create trust and credibility[9]. Unfortunately, leaders always fail to match words with actions on the issues of employee involvement in the decision-making processes[9].

Effective leadership in public organizations should always develop the strategies that create the enabling environment for high involvement leadership that evolves through employee empowerment. The empowerment strategies should involve creating mutually agreed targets; and expanding job roles and responsibilities, whenever necessary.

Developing relevant skills (Developing Employees)

For more effectiveness, leaders of public organizations should always be future-oriented. This is very necessary as future-oriented organizations tend to employ progressive human resource practices; in which the emphasis is on assessing the knowledge, skills and abilities needed for the future; as well as on instituting staffing appraisal and evaluation on incentive and compensation; and on training and developmental programs[4]. Identifying the crucial competences and training of the employees is of utmost importance. Even the leaders should possess human, technical, and conceptual skills[10].

There should also be a constant and overriding need to invest in human development. Ultimately, the final goal of strategic human resources of any organization should be to support, manage and maintain high-commitment and high-performance employees[3]. This becomes imperative as the employees of an organization can be a source for sustained advantage; which can determine the ultimate success of the organization[18]. Moreover, "given the importance of people in organizations, most strategic human resource departments should consider the management of the competencies and capabilities of these human assets as the primary goals[19].

Leadership should be viewed as an organizational competence; which everyone in the organization should not only possess, but should always continuously develop[1a]. An organization, which regards leadership as an organizational competence supports leadership development and educational programs for all its employees.

Learning Organization (Leadership as Learning Process)

To respond to the changing environment, the leadership of a public organization must possess an understanding of the relationship between effective learning strategies and leadership. Organizational learning is comprehendable as processes of identifying formation, skills, and information; as well as their acquisitions[15]. To become a learning organization, there is need to create an appreciative inquiry process; which is describable as a tool that helps learning organizations engage in meaningful dialogue to uncover forces of positive change. The concept of appreciative inquiry requires that organizations make commitment to continuous learning, growth, and generative changes[22]. That there is a strong relationship between effective leadership and learning suggests that leadership is essentially, a learning process[20].

Feedback Mechanism

Leaders are trusted more by their followers if they encourage open two-way communication, and share information[7]. As an open-door policy can also serve as an effective feedback system, leadership must design and implement one. This can be achieved through open communication systems that encourage employee feedback; as well as facilitate a two-way flow of information[12]. Leaders should know and understand their subordinates, know what they believe and value, and also act on their values and beliefs through open and honest communication with them[1].

Providing ethical Leadership

To optimize their competences, leadership of public organizations must place more emphasis on integrity. This should be understandable as, ethically speaking, the credibility of a public organization lies on its integrity[2]. In public organizations, the general assumption is that justice is applied through rules and regulations. Some public organizations do not, however, draw up codes of ethics for their employees. These organizations do not have formal statement of the company's values concerning ethics and social responsibilities. To ensure the prevalence of high ethical standards, public organizations should have internal ombudsmen who act as the 'organizational conscience'; investigating ethical complaints; as well as ensuring adherence to professional and organizational ethics.

PATH VI

STRATEGIC DECISION-MAKING and PLANNING for PUBLIC ORGANIZATIONS

Chapter 21

Frameworks for Strategic Decision-Making

Decision making in a public organization can be described as a process by which courses of action are selected from multiple alternatives, toward the pursuit of organizational and public goals[1]. From this perpective, decision making in public organizations can be assessed as the patterns of communications and relationships in a group; which provides each member with information, goals, and attitudes that come to bear on his or her decisions.

Four models can be used to conduct or analyze decision making in public organizations. These four perspectives are the rational choice model, the bureaucratic model, the organizational processs model, and the government politics model. The rational choice model is mostly used when the situations and issues are only within the organization. The bureaucratic model is used when previous rules and processes have been found to be effective. The organizational process model is most appropriate when the situations or issues invovle multiple organizations or departments. The government politics model is used when there are competing interests, as in such cases as when government departments reconcile their different and competing interests in budgetary allocations; in multi-level negotiations; or in international negotiations.

The Rational Choice Model
This describes a decision-making model, in which goals are first

clearly defined; and then the levels of achievements of the goals that would be considered satisfactory are set out[2]. The model assumes that organizational events are purposeful choices made out of consistent actions[3]. This model therefore, assumes that behaviours within organizations are not accidental or randon; rather, they reflect intentions or purposes that pre-exist, and hence guide organizational behaviours[3].

This rational choice model also assumes that there is a unity of purpose or that the chosen preferences, objectives, or goals characterize the particular organization[3]. The model, not only presumes that the goals and objectives of the chosen lines of action characterize the organization; but it also presummes that the rationality cannot be defined or assesssed except from the perspective of these goals or objectives. In this model, the decision making processes are mobilized in defined strategic ways toward the goals and objectives.

As this model focuses on organizational goals; and the strategies to reach the goals, it starts with the assumption of a goal or consistent set of goals. Then, all the alternatives goals are canvassed, and systematically compared in terms of costs and benefits[2]. Then again, the choice is made of the alternative that would achieve the goals at the least costs.

The rational choice model can be constituted in phases that include: the pre-analysis phase, the analytical phase, the design phase, the choice phase, and the implementation phase. In the pre-analysis phase, the situations/problems are thoroughly defined from the perspectives of the goals and objectives of the organization. Identifying the problems is a critical step in decision-making. The strategic leader must carefully evaluate such issues as the performance sytem, the alternative service providers, laws and regulations; the needs and desires of the citizens; and any other pertinent factors; all in attempts to locate problems within the organization. Identifying the problems that deter and inhibit the potentials of the organization will, however, largely depend on the leader's ability to find or anticipate these problems.

In the analytical phase, the problems/situations that affect the goals are analyzed and information about them are gathered and processed. This usually entails a thorough analysis of the internal and external problems that affect the performance of the organization. The problem analysis can include such issues as; the changing demographics, diversity issues, manpower issues, reduction in statutory or budget allocatios, new technologies and innovations; as well as changes in legislative mandates.

In the design phase, the alternatives/options to deal with the problems/situations are developed and concisely laid out. The information on these alternatives is obtained through search processes. The search has to be conducted until satisfactory alternatives are found. Once a set of alternatives (whether few or many), have been found, assessments are made of the likely outcomes of the various courses of action associable with each alternative. These possible outcomes would also include the risks and uncertainties associated with each course of action.

Risk assessment involves the determination of the possible unforeseen outcomes arising from a decision or action, and evaluating how likely it is that one or more of the unwanted events would occur. Risks are hazardous and uncertain, but such a tool as risk forecasting is usually employed to minimize the uncertainty. On a brighter side, risks can be regarded as opportunities, as trying to understand the risks involved in an alternative could create opportunities for innovation and new initiative.

In the choice phase, the alternatives/options are evaluated and the optimal choice is made. As the model requires that goals be consistent, the next step becomes how to choose the set of decision-making alternatives that are differentiable from one another. Using the risks and uncertainties associated with each alternative, the estimates of the probability of the occurrence of various consequences are used to assess the values of the consequences of the alternatives. At this stage, it can be safely assumed that all the consequences can now be fully assessed and anticipated; although there may be some degree of uncertainty. At this stage also, everything that can possibly occur has been specified. The rational choice becomes that of selecting the course of action (or alternative) that maximizes the likelihood of the organization in attaining the desired highest values as defined or guided by its organizational goals or objectives.

In the implementation phase, the chosen alternative is carried out. The success of any chosen alternative will depend on its translation into action. Sometimes this never happens; especially, when the leadership lacks the resources, energy, or commitment required to translate this into action.

In this model, the phases are deliberately performed with reliance on the rationality of the decision makers[1]. The rationality entails that the concerned individuals will work toward making value-maximizing choices. The assumptions on which this model is built are that decisions are orderly, intentional, purposeful, deliberate, consistent, responsible, accountable, explainable, and rational[1]. An advantage of this model is, hence, that it is an attractive way of thinking and analyzing organizational problems. More often, however, a single executive or his or her delegates make the rational choice. There is therefore, the need to be on the watch for the tendency for protecting or promoting self-interest as is possible in this model.

Another advantage is that it allows the prediction of organization behaviour with high level of certainty; as long as the goals of the organization are known. Under unanticipated crisis from external actors, for instance, this model could also be used to make sense of the reason, intentions, and motivations of the external actors; and can assist in the deliberate analysis and calculations of the consequences of various outcomes. The model can, hence, facilitate the prediction of what and how other organizations can act; if their goals are known. The model of decision making is therefore, popular among such top spy agencies as America's Central Intelligence Agency (CIA), Russia's Federal Security Service (FSB-successor to KGB), Britain's Foreign Intelligence Service (MI6), Israel's National Intelligence Agency (Mossad), and France's General Directorate for External Security (DGSE- *Direction générale de la sécurité extérieure)*.

A criticism of this model is that the personal values and feelings of the decision-makers play important part in the decision making. Also, moral values, which do not have anything to do with rationality, could guide behaviors of decision-makers[1]. Moreover, the concept of bounded rationality holds that persons usually have limited resources to put into search activitites; as well as limited capacities to process the found information[3]. As the bounded rationality concept portends; since costs are associated with the search processes, larger number of alternatives may not be considered. This need for the processing of substantial information as required in this model of decision-making sometimes makes it unrealistic or unattainable; especially to small or less well-funded public organizations.

The Bureaucratic Model

The bureaucratic model of decision-making replaces the procedural rationality of the rational choice model with substantive rationality[3]. That is, it replaces decision-making by rational procedures with decision-making by rational substance. Rather than making choices to maximize values as required by the rational choice model, the bureaucratic model makes choices in accordance with rules and processes that have be found to be effective in the past[3].

As in the rational choice models, goals are also first clearly defined; and then the levels of satisfactory achievements of the goals set out. Similarly, this model also presumes that the goals and objectives of the chosen lines of action characterize the organization; and that the rationality cannot be assesssed except from the perspective of the goals or objectives. In this model, the decision must also satisfy the goals.

In contrast, however, because of the associated costs defined by the bounded rationality, the search processes in this bureaucratic model are not unlimited; and therefore, searching is stopped as soon as a satisfactory alternative is found. In additon, rather than making comprehensive assessments of risks and their probabilities; decisions are made quickly because conflicts between various alternatives are not fully resolved as objectives are prioritized and sequentially attended to. In essence, this model tends to encourage the acceptance of the first satisfactory alternative that is uncovered, rather than maximizing or searching until the optimal alternative is determined.

As the organization learns and adapts their learning, the knowledge now becomes the rules of action or the standard operating procedure[3]. Obviously, decisions are not made as deliberate choices; but are rather made in accordance with standard patterns of behaviour; which had been determined by previously established procedures[3]. The model is most appropriate for use by small or less well-funded public organizations.

This model has the presumption of less foresighting and less clearly defined preferences as it relies on habitual ways of doing thing; as well as on the results of past actions. The model, therefore, constraints the organization on how it proceeds in its future operations and endeavours. The model also presumes that there are no overall organizational goals that have to be maximized through choices.

The Organizational Process Model

This model, as an alternative to the rational model, views governments as consisting of loosely allied organizations; each with its own set of leaders who possess and display different behaviors[1]. This model focuses, not on single individual organization, but on the loose alliance of semi-independent organizations; each operating according to set standards of operating procedures. One individual leader cannot completely control the process; thereby, creating the possibility of multiple agents in the decision-making process. To accomplish any complex tasks, the behaviors of these different individuals must be coordinated[1].

Under this model, the decision makers from the various organizations are required to first develop a set of standard operating procedures. Then, the various organizations take whatever they are currently doing as given; and then make incremental adjustments toward the new predetermined goals or visions, using the set of standard operating procedures. In this model, the organizational outcomes are more predictable as decision makers are contrained by the standard operating procedures[1].

This model avoids situations in which the various organizations spend resources and time; defining multiple goals, canvassing a multitude of alternatives, doing a magnitude of comparisons, and probably working at cross purposes. This model is therefore, most appropriate when decisions are to be made by multiple organizations toward predetermined visions or goals. Its appropriateness lies on the requirement that the multiple organizations make incremental changes in accordance with the standard operating precedures. The model is most appropriate when multiple public organizations face similar external challenges or are required to act in unison to tackle a common societal problem. A typical example is the department of homeland security, the state troopers, the Federal Bureau of Investigation (FBI), and the Refugee Processing Center (RPC) attempting to tackle the refugee crisis that occured on the southern border of the United States in 2014.

Another example would be in tackling the threat of terrorism as a common problem in the United States. The National Counter-terrorism Center (NCTC), the Federal Bureau of Investigations (FBI), the Central Intelligence Agency (CIA), local police departments, and such local first responders as fire service would have to cooperate and work together to make decisions as they map out the counter-terrorism strategies or responses.

The Government Process Model

Unlike the rational model in which a single executive can make the rational choice; decisions in the government process model are group efforts that involve bargaining among organizations with different and competing interests[1]. This model involves multiple decision makers; each with its own agenda, priorities, and time tables. This model recognizes complex and multiple issues being considered by different organizations; with their different multiple interests and agenda, and operating in different social and political spheres. Like the organizational process model, the problems may be common; but in contrast, the various organizations (or nations) come with their own agenda, priorities, and time. The decisions from this model are outcomes of bargaining, rather than outcomes of single rational choices.

This model entails that distinct organizations or entities with separate objectives, but with shared power over the processes, arrive at decisions by means of collegial bargaining[1]. Each organization is influenced by its position, perceptions, practices, and priorities; and how the agenda is set is critical in explainig decisions and outcomes.

Under this model, decisions could be reached by resolution in which problems are resolved after some period of time has been spent working on them.

This is the decision model usually adopted by such multi-lateral organizations as the United Nations and its organs in the conduct of their negotiations. Such public institutions as the United States department of State usually adopt this model when negotiating with other countries. This model is tailor-made for such international negotiations as the Iranian nuclear deal between Iran and the 5P plus 1 group (the 5 permanent members of the United Nations security Council-United States, Britain, Russia, France, and China; plus Germany).

Chapter 22

Techniques for Decision-Making

Having decided on the decision model to adopt, namely; either the rational choice model, bureaucratic model, organizational processs model, or the government politics model; a public organization will also need to gather the information, make the decisions, and in the course of time, evaluate the decisions. There are approaches to information gathering that includes the use of focus groups and brainstorming. The various alternative solutions generated are evaluated through the cost-benefit analysis techniques, and then the decisions that have been made are, with time, evaluated through the techniques of cost-effectiveness analysis.

Information Gathering

Like Individuals, organizations are limited in their decision-making as they sometimes act on incomplete information; thereby exploring alternatives that have been grossly limited. In all the models for decision-making, recognizing and identifying a problem and gathering the required information are the first steps in problem solving and decision making[1]. As the bounded rationality concept indicates, there are usually costs associated with information searching processes. For public organizations, the information needed for decision-making can be gathered by means of a focus group or brainstorming; and evaluated through cost-benefit analysis or/and cost-effectiveness analysis.

Focus Groups

This is an approach for receiving the input of large number of individuals in order to facilitate the decision making process[1]. Typically, focus groups usually consist of about 20 people or less, who are informed and conversant with the issues of concern; and who discuss these issues under the guidance of a researcher or trained facilitator. Any information gathered from the focus group is analyzed and used in the decision-making process.

The core steps for setting up a focus group are: (i) planning, during which the major decisions to be made are spelt out; (ii) recruiting the appropriate and suitable participants; and (iii) analysis, in which the information obtained from the participants is analyzed and reported. Essentially, the information gathered from the focus group is used for problem identification, planning, implementation, or assessments.

Brainstorming

Brainstorming is used to generate large number of ideas within a short time frame. This is one of the most widely used approaches, and is typically used to create ideas and generate alternatives; as well as foster creativity[1]. The major concept behind this approach is to increase the creative thinking that helps to generate solutions without the inhibitions and interrruptions usually created by criticisms[1].

The key steps to brainstorming are: (i) stating the problems clearly, but not concisely, and without restrictions; (ii) stating the ground rules that indicate that there shall no judgements on generated ideas; as the greater the quantity of ideas, the better; and (iii) generating the ideas, using the ground rules.

A facilitator ensures adherence to the ground rules whose major essence is to generate as many ideas as possible for creative solutions to the problems. Focus groups can also be used in conjuction with brainstorming, or to analyze the ideas generated by brainstorming.

Evaluation and Choice Making

When some information and creative ideas have been gathered through brainstorming or focus grouping, the next step would be to assess the various alternative solutions. Some analytical tools available for these assessments are the cost-benefit and cost-effectiveness techniques.

Cost-Benefit Analysis

The cost-benefit technique is used by public organizations and government agencies to plan programs, allocate resources, and evaluate outcomes[1]. The approach is used by these public organizations and government agencies to identify and quantify both the adverse impacts (costs) and the beneficial impacts (benefits) of a proposed or ongoing project; and by subtracting one from the other, determine the net benefits, expressed in monetary terms[1].

Although, this approach is appropriate for assessing programme efficiency in terms of money, it is noteworthy that government programs are also underlined by social costs. As social equity entails fairness in the delivery of public services, each citizen has the right to equal treatment under the political system. To effectively evaluate those programs that have social costs or other non-monetary costs or items, it is always necessary to use the cost-effectiveness analysis.

Cost-Effectiveness Analysis

This is an analytical technique that is used to measure the effectiveness of the public programmes that do have non-monetary items. The approach is used to compare the outputs of a programme to the cost of the programme[1]. Whereas the cost of the programme would consist of such costs as personnel, facilities, or equipments; the output would be the stated goals and objectives of the program. The cost is compared with how the programme goals and objectives are met, especially with regard to possible alternatives.

The key steps for this analysis are; (i) identifying the objectives of a work/service activity in the programme; (ii) determining the criteria for assessing whether or not the objectives are met; (iii) examining the current cost of the work/service activity; (iv) examining the current level of quality of the work/service activity; (v) based on information on the cost and quality of activity, as well as ways activity is performed, identify and develop alternative ways of performing activity; and using the new procedures to assess cost and service quality effects of each alternative; and (vi) if necessary, adjust work activity to reflect new cost and quality.

Chapter 23

Strategic Planning for Optimizing Leadership

Strategic planning can be viewed as the process of making concise decisions on the objectives of an organization; preparing for possible changes in these objectives, and marshalling out the resources required for the attainment of these objectives; as well as determining what will guide the acquisition and use of these resoiurces. Strategic planning can also be described as the periodic actions and activities an organization embarks on, in order to cope with changes in its environment[4]. Strategic planning is designed to direct an organization's objectives and visions[11]. Another purpose of strategic planning is to turn the goals of the organization into realities within a definite period of time[4]. The philosophy of strategic planning essentially links goals with day-to-day decision making; creating a fit between an organization's external and internal environments[10]. Strategic planning consitutes the means of understanding change within an organization; and helping the organization control its future[5]. While change is inevitable; it is bound to happen especially in this day and age with technology is advancing rapidly. Strategic planning can, therefore, be used as a tool for change.

In public organizations, strategic planning can be used as the blueprint that defines the organizational activities and the resource allocations required for attaining future goals[4]. Using strategic planning, these organizations can be focused on defining the steps by which they intend to attain these future goals. Strategic planning can, hence, also be described as the process by which priorities are

133

established on what a public organization will accomplish in the future. For public organization, therefore, the strategic planning process should be an "ongoing process"; as well as a cornerstone of all the businesses conducted within the organizations.

Strategic Planning

As means of understanding change within and outside the organization, strategic planning helps a public organization control its future. With strategic planning, public organizations are able to create a one to ten year road map for organizational development and growth; only requiring minor changes at some milestones of its development[5]. Effective strategic planning involves environmental analysis; formulation of long-tem objectives and roadmaps; strategic analysis and choice; and plans and implementation. Generally, strategic planning involves developing a roadmap for those major decisions, and actions that could, in their entireties, chart the course of organizations. Although, this involves the analysis of internal and external; it is the formulation and implementation of the strategies that make public services citizenry-oriented.

Strategic planning for public organizations essentially requires looking forward critically at how future events could potentially impact the organization; and how the organization's leaders should prepare for, and address future changes; if and when they occur[5]. The strategic plan should encompass both a process and a product that is thought provoking and introspective; and is comprehensive of key issues; as well as the solutions for those issues[5].

Strategic planning allows the public organization to set forth policy, rules, and regulations. A good strategic plan points out individual responsibilities, expectancies, and disciplinary actions. It also enables public organizations implement good practices; and deal with situations and/or circumstances that go against policy, rules, and regulations.

Public organizations are expected to deliver high-quality services at less cost with their ever shrinking revenue sources; even with unforeseen external changes and public emergencies. Having such plans for the unexpected will always result in a better response and quicker resolutions[5].

Public organizations are, however, usually slower than the private organizations in embracing strategic planning principles. This is due to the traditional focus of the public sectors on their functions, rather than on objectives[10]. This should no longer absolutely be the case, especially for the reasons of the rapid pace of changes taking place in the served communities of the public organizations. Obviously, the cross movement of staff between the public and private sectors is leading to the cross-breeding of ideas between the two sectors. Such concepts as Management by Objectives (MBO) and strategic planning that once seemed as the exclusive preserves of the private sectors are gradually creeping into the management "tool bags" of the public organizations.

It has, however, been argued that the step-by-step decision making processes are more appropriate than strategic planning for the public organizations in multi-democratic systems[9]. This so-called "incrementalism" model may be appropriate for stable and wealthy democracies like the United States; developing countries with their enormous problems would need more strategic planning[10].

For most public organizations, there could still be some elements of incremental decision making; especially, in those areas that do not lend themselves to long-term planning; such as budget proposals and implementation. On the other hand, in such sectors as energy, education, and health that are enhanced by long-term objectives, strategic planning is most appropriate. Obviously, leaders of public organizations who do not on their own, design and adopt internal policies that would align with the ever-changing demands and expectations of the customers (citizens) run the risks of undergoing drastic legislatively-imposed reforms.

Success Elements in Strategic Planning

The key elements for a successful strategic planning include: environmental scanning; sharing and collaboration; review by experts; performanace budgeting, team decision making, performance appraisal, effective implementation, strategic control mechanisms, feedback mechanism, and effective leadership.

Environmental Analysis

Environmental analysis involves the collation of the relevant data and analysis of such data as they affect functions and responsibilities in the organization. An effective environmental analysis program enables the decision maker understand the current and potential changes taking place in the external environments. This analysis usually provides the tactical and strategic intelligence needed for the determination of organizational strategy. There is always the profound need for public organizations to create and retain the required tactical and strategic intelligence; by constantly scanning and analyzing their environments.

Effective Implementation Planning

The environmental analysis is followed by the development of the strategic direction that the implementation process would follow. This roadmap should indicate the strategic direction of the organization and the resources needed to get to the desired destination. The implementation process essentially involves putting the short-term objectives into action by first communicating the plans and strategies to the employees; and the allocation of resources to the processes. Technical skills are especially relevant to the effective and efficient implementation of the strategic plan[1].

The critical factors that are necessary for a successful plan implementation are the development and adoption of the strategies and goals that conform to the objectives; and the ability to communicate them to the employees. In addition, it is necessary that the organization prepares and plans in advance. This is very necessary as preparation and planning tend to create and elevate the implementation processes to a higher level of certainty.

In the implementation of the planning processes, it may recommendable to: (i) identify the major deliverables, (ii) tie spending plans to major deliverables, rather than time, (iii) expend the monetary resources step-by-step, rather than up-front, (iv) decide in advance the criteria for adjusting the plans, and (v) set up a monitoring system.

Sharing and Collaboration

Strategic planning is not simply designed to bring people together to take a detailed look at what is going on in the organization; it is a critical assessment of the direction in which an organization chooses to proceed in the future. A strategic planning system must include the voices of as many people as possible; both within and outside the organization. For any plan to be successful, the stakeholders must believe in the visions spelt out in the strategic plan. The organizational leaders must garner the buy-in of the stakeholders; because without it, there could be a lack of support.

Collaboration must, however, first begin within the organization. By including as many employees as possible in the planning process, the employees are inspired in the quality of their efforts and commitment to the implementation of the strategic plan[7]. In budget planning for instance, the progression of discussions from line-item budgets to programme budgeting; and the more recent move to performance budgeting must involve inputs from all the units and departments within the organization. This enables the overall expenditures to be linked to both the unit and organizational objectives.

Review by Experts

As the strategic plans are developed, the leadership of public organizations must rely on the knowledge of the subject matter experts. The leadership must put aside their parochial interests; approaching the environmental scanning, the identification of issues, and the development of goals and tactics with an eye on the best interests of the organization, rather than on their own narrower interest[5]. Leaders must always remain aware of their personal biases, values, and beliefs; and act in the best interest of the organization as opposed to advancing their careers at the cost of the organizational interests. To avoid personal biases and the bolstering of their narrow interests, leaders must seek the counsel and opinions of the subject matter experts.

Performance Budgeting

Traditionally, a budget is a financial plan that expresses the goals and objectives of management; while also serving as a tool to control future operations and results[11]. Strategic planning shares a relationship with budgeting as it provides guidance for the budget. As such, budgeting can also be described as the formalization of the strategic planning process[11].

A performance budgeting system, however, focuses on identifying service delivery inputs, outputs, and departmental outcomes. Goals, objectives, and strategies must, therefore, be tied to a performance budgeting system. These benchmarks, namely; service delivery inputs, outputs, and departmental outcomes, must be linked to departmental performance, budget priorities, and financial allocations. Otherwise, for fear of reduction in budgets, departments will seek to spend unnecessarily; thereby focusing efforts on the departments, rather than on their roles in the overall accomplishment of the organizational strategic plan.

As most public officers would have noticed; at the end of the fiscal year, there is always this race to spend whatever money that still remains in the budget. This is why most public organizations focus on spending all the money in their budgets without seeking to increase organizational performance and efficiency.

Team Decision-Making

The manner in which an organization makes decisions affects both the development of the strategic plan and its implementation[5]. Described as the hybrid of the top-down (senior management as the driving force) and the bottom-up (emphasis on those who are involved in daily operations) styles of decision making; team-decision making process encourage broader representation and consideration of wide array of matters[5].

Gathering information from line employees allows and prepares leadership and management for any necessary changes in organizational policies, rules, and regulations. It also provides shared knowledge to management of the citizens' impacts and concerns; which can help in the improvement and growth of the organization. This approach has always proven effective as senior and middle managers, as well as the technical cadre all contribute in their different areas of expertise. Team decision making approach to the crafting of strategic plans is appropriate for public organizations.

Performance Appraisal

Performance appraisal is the ongoing process of evaluating employee's performance[3]. The purposes of performance appraisal include: providing opportunities for formal communication between organizational leaders and subordinates on their levels of performance; allowing management to evaluate employees, and providing motivation to employees. The performance appraisal process involves job analysis, the development of standards, and adoption of measurement standards.

In developing the performance appraisal instruments, the rating elements can include; initiative, output, attendance, attitude, cooperation, quality of work, quantity of work, or dependability. The three specific types of performance appraisal instruments are: (i) graphic rating scale, (ii) the comparative techniques, and (iii) the behaviorally anchored rating scale.

Graphic rating scale

Graphic rating scale comes in different formats; and is the most widely used performance appraisal instrument[3]. This appraisal instrument chooses the most descriptive or evaluative rating from a range of possibilities. In this performance appraisal instrument, employees are rated on such continuum of performance as poor, fair, average, good, and excellent or on a numerical scale as 1(lowest performance)-5(highest performance). The rating scales can also be on such range as; unsatisfactory, fair, satisfactory, good, and outstanding.

Comparative techniques

These are performance appraisal instruments in which the performance of an employee is appraised against the performance of others. The instruments of these techniques include; ranking, paired comparison, and forced distribution. In the ranking technique, job performance is ranked from the highest to the lowest. The paired comparison analysis enables comparison to be made between relevant options. In forced distribution, employee performances are ranked in forced allocation of levels of performances as, for example, 10% of employees in the highest level, 80% in the middle, and 10% in the lowest.

Behaviorally anchored rating scale (BARS)

A performance appraisal instrument can also be based on behaviorally anchored rating scale; in which standards are defined by typical instances of behavior as they correspond to different possible ratings. This appraisal instrument provides the descriptions of each assessment of an employee along a continuum. An example of BARS is the rubric used in some colleges in which the difference between excellent (A), good (B), Average (C), Poor (D), and Not acceptable (F) are described in details.

Strategic Control Mechanisms

Strategic control mechanisms are used as performance measures to determine if the organization is on track, or needs corrective actions[5]. Strategic control is essentially the evaluation of whether or not a strategy is being implemented as intended; and whether or not the desired results are being achieved. If not, corrective actions may be required to modify the implementation activities or even the strategy itself.

Strategic planning efforts are most effective when they are continuous and recurring[7]. Strategic controls create the means of validating and adjusting the strategies by ensuring that operations are monitored to detect deviations. Strategic control usually focuses on two questions; is the strategy being implemented as planned? If yes, is the strategy producing the intended results?

Feedback Mechanisms

An effective feedback mechanism brings problems to the attention of leadership; for instance, programmes that are not working as planned, or implementation that does not square with their interpretation to the legislative mandate[6]. The leadership, which has set the goals and made the decisions, gets the feedback; and then changes or modifies the course of actions.

Responding to the feedbacks and making timely and appropriate adjustments are important. Although, it is true that organizations tend to resist change, feedback or evaluation frequently leads to incremental changes or improvements in the design and administration of programmes. Strategic planning should, therefore, include re-planning and adjusting courses of action in light of new information or developments arising from the feedbacks. An effective feedback mechanism enables the strategic planning process to go full circle; with the evaluative information creating new agenda item for subsequent decisions. Creating feedback loops are critical to the success of a strategic plan.

Effective Leadership

Strategic planning is a process made up of interactions between people, who are supposed to work toward a common vision and purpose; and which, when combined, results in demonstrable value.

Strategic planning, however, requires, a leadership that generates a vision of a compelling future; the communication of that vision and future; and at least an implementable system of execution, inside of which the actions to bring that future into reality can actually occur[7]. It is this vision of leadership that links strategic planning with day-to-day decision making.

For instance, transformational leaders can be good for strategic management purposes, because they are visionaries in a sense, and can also look toward change as being beneficial to the organization; which then, creates opportunities for growth[8]. The required leadership skills would include the ability to; recognize, harness, and inspire the organization's workforce for the execution of the plan. Coordinating these skills emphasizes the need for the leadership that can align the interests of all the stakeholders toward the common purposes.

PART VII

PUBLIC ORGANIZATIONS:

ETHICS, VALUES, and NATIONAL CULTURES

Chapter 24

Ethics and Values in Public Organizations

Values can be defined as the strongly held preferences or standards that guide the conduct of people[1]. Values are essentially those concepts which individuals, cultures, or communities hold as true. They are the "moral compass that guide us" in our decisions. Values can help us determine between right and wrong, and can help us to set priorities[7]. Values include such concepts that border on love, family, religion, brotherhood, individualism, community, or equality[4]. Values are important for individuals, organizations, and governments; but they are useless unless they are practiced[7]. To be constructive, values must be transformed into action.

Ethics, on the other hand, are rules of personal conducts[4]. Ethics involve behaviours that are concerned with acting on the right values or doing the right thing[3]. Ethics are about right and wrong, good and bad, benefit and harm; and they define the nature of public managers, leaders, and administrators[13]. Ethical issues are values that directly relate to beliefs concerning what is right and proper, as opposed to what is simply correct or effective or that motivates a sense of moral duty. Such transcedent values as justice, truth, and fairness are those characteristics we generally view as ethical behaviors.

Essentially, ethics are standards of right and wrong; while values are more specific beliefs about life, love, family, time-use, and religion. Ethics refer to standards of conduct that indicate how one should behave based on moral duties and virtues; whereas, values are those core beliefs or desires that guide or motivate attitudes and actions. Obviously, some difficulties still exist in distinguishing between ethics and values, especially, in terms of their relationships to cultural differences.

At the center of ethics is the behavior of individuals. Its scope, however, is broader as people may make judgments based on personal standards; whereas institutions define and control situations in which decisions are made[13]. As individuals are at the center of ethical decisions, the reactions of public organization are usually the fatal choices[14]. Ethics involve three kinds of thinking: descriptive, normative, and critical; all of which are relevant to the field of ethics[10].

In democratic governance, as sovereinty belongs to the people, it is imperative that public officials regard themselves as servants, and not masters of the people. The power belongs to the people; and as such, public officials must regard their powers as delegated and temporary. A public organization belongs to all citizens, and those who work for and are paid by the organization are ultimately servants of the whole citizenry[11]. Although public officials are bound by the same criminal laws as applicable to other citizens, their obligations to public and the concepts of public trust bestows additional and more rigorous set of ethical standards on them[11].

Influence of Cultures on Ethics and Values

Cultures and nationalities are important because we all derive our identities from them; and our thinking is partly conditioned by our culture. It is this cultural orientation that guides the individual's values, work ethics, and morality. Each culture has its own norms, values, and conception of justice. In a given society, there are clearly many perspectives from which one can look at any issue; and there are many perceptions about those different perspectives.

Essentially, the differences in the cultural orientation distinguish one individual from another. Like spirituality, people form opinions and hold beliefs that differ from one culture to another. The specific ethical or moral principles are what define a cultural group's identity. It is noteworthy, however, that although, the behaviors of the individual are partially pre-determined by collective programming, such individuals can still react in ways different from their culture[12].

As ethical standards can also be imposed by the society, it differs from one society to the other. In analyzing these cross-cultural variations with respect to ethical perceptions, moral judgments, and ethical beliefs; the Hofstede's two dimensions, namely; the power distance and the level of masculinity have the tendencies to affect ethical dispositions[6].

In high power distance societies such as Pakistan, Saudi Arabia, India, Turkey, Thailand, Nigeria, Venezuela, Malaysia, Mexico, and the Philippines, much respect is shown for authorities, titles, birth and religious status; and a great deal of importance is also attached to status and rank. Paternalism is a very common leadership style in these countries. The leaders are expected to make decisions autocratically and paternalistically; and subordinates are generally afraid and unwilling to disagree with them[5]. In the past, the paternalistic disposition of these societies created a culture of paying homage to local leaders, kings and chiefs. In modern times, this culture of paying homage has somewhat translated to high incidence and tolerance for gratifications to the political and bureaucratic leadership. In such societies, there is much tolerance for unethical behavior of your bosses and political leadership.

In high masculinity societies as most Arab countries, there is much gender-bias; as different sets of laws apply to the males and females. Due to this gender apartheid, women are excluded from certain environments, separated at public places; and are not allowed to drive and are generally discriminated against. The cultural justification for not allowing women to drive in Saudi Arabia is merely on the grounds that unsupervised movement of individual women; whenever and wherever they want to go, will encourage sexual misconduct[2]. The law forbids women to work in environments where they would be in the company of men[9]; leading to gender segregation in the workplaces. Generally, women are not permitted to be in the company of men who are not immediate relatives or husbands.

The United Nations convention on the Elimination of All forms of Discrimination against Women (CEDAW) is against such practices. Adopted in 1979 by the UN General Assembly, and often described as an international bill of rights for women, the

Convention defines discrimination against women as "...any distinction, exclusion or restriction made on the basis of sex which has the effect or purpose of impairing or nullifying the recognition, enjoyment or exercise by women, irrespective of their marital status, on a basis of equality of men and women, of human rights and fundamental freedoms in the political[9]. Saudi Arabia also discriminates against its black citizens; who constitute about ten percentages of the country's population. Among the numerous degrading and humiliating treatments the black citizens of Saudi Arabia experience include not being allowed to hold government jobs. These situations have always presented serious ethical dilemmas for foreigners living or working in Saudi Arabia; especially those from countries that have codified gender and racial non-discrimination. The difficulty in making ethical decisions is, therefore, often exacerbated on the international front due to the different value systems and practices.

Different Cultural Scenerios of Ethics

Not only are there differences between cultures; each culture changes over time, and that affects the values of that culture[8]. Some three typical scenarios can be used to explain the relationship of ethics and values as they vary in different cultures. A first scenario presents firm ethical "laws" that govern our behavior; irrespective of cultures and values. These laws, which span across all cultures and values, are based strictly on the ethical "laws". All behaviors are determined to be right or wrong based on the ethical "laws". Most declarations of the United Nations, such as the United Nations Declaration of Human rights, and rights of women and children are based on this scenerio. In this scenerio, it can be deduced that values are determined and espoused on the basis of universal ethics.

In a second scenario, the societal ethics are based on the values of its culture. In this case, ethics change within each culture. Behaviors are judged as right or wrong, based on the values; and subsequently the ethics of that culture. In thisscenerio, the cultural values determine ethics. Some cultures, for instance, encourage or allow discrimination of individuals with diverse sexual orientation, or condone such violence against women as beatings or clitoral

146

circumcision[8]. While these practices are acceptable in some societies, they are not in others. In this scenario, ethics are relative; as culture determines what is right or wrong. Under this scenerio, Western values for instance, would be considered no better than those of other cultures[8]. These cultural differences always make ethical decisions more difficult for international managers and people who are called upon to lead in 'strange lands'[7].

A third scenario, in which there are basic ethical principles; yet each culture, has a variety of values that make it unique. Behaviors are considered right or wrong based on either these basic ethical principles, or on the values of the culture. In this scenario, basic ethics are constant, while the values vary. Although, the values can differ, some behaviors would be considered to be out of bounds even if some individuals in some cultures engage in them[8].

In today's global environment, more organizational leaders struggle with ethical decisions as cultural values continue to vary in work environments. In distinguishing between ethics and values in relationship with cultural differences, one must consider the implications of ethical decisions on the society and its values. In a global environment, it becomes incumbent upon the organizational leader to understand these cultural differences whenever issues of ethics and values arise.

Although, within a particular country, leaders and managers of public organizations also have personal values that may be based on religious beliefs, family background, heritage, or ethnicity; they must interpret these values, and act in ways that are reasonably and objectively ethical. Their actions should also be based on the ethics of their fields of practice; regardless of any particular cultural influences. In the context of a country, it would be merely ethnocentric for any individual to believe that his or her values and ethics are what could be called "perfectly all right"; particularly when facing situations that introduce other facts or issues into their perspective[14].

Although, participants in public leadership do need to be culturally sensitive, they however, also need to balance the culutral sentivity with basic objective of discerning right from wrong, or good from evil. Leaders in public organizations should be open-minded to the extent that they are capable of questioning the values or ethics of their own cultures, and hence, becoming capable of broadening their viewpoints; enabling them to incorporate sound reasoning into their actions[14]. The role of the public leader is, therefore, to objectify values and ethics regardless of any cultural viewpoints[14]. Invariably, organizational leaders have to balance competing pressures in their dealings with ethics, legality, and fairness[3].

Chapter 25

General Ethical Perspectives for Public Organizations

Ethics in public leadership are primarily about how our actions affect other people. Usually, issues of ethics tend to exist in virtually most public decision-making processes. Ethical dilemmas arise when right or wrong cannot be clearly identified; and each alternative has a potentially harmful ethical consequence. Issues of ethics have assumed bigger dimension because interactions between the government and the governed have become more frequent; and activities and decisions are no longer absolutely governed by primordial interests. Other reasons include; the increasing scope of legislative enactments, and the public concern about such public issues as child labor, sexual harrassment in workplaces, pollution, climate change, racial and gender discrimination, economic exploitation, and workplace safety.

Generally, most ethical decisions in public organizations involve a conflict between the interests of the individuals and government policies; or between the public organization and the society. Should war prisoners be tortured? Should the environmental pollution tendencies of company be left to take precedence over the job it creates for a needy community? To solve these ethical problems, does one have to rely on the norms and values of the corporation or those of the society?

The issues of ethics should be those of social responsibility; the organizational leadership must determine its legislated responsibilities and its allegiance to the political leadership; and decide how to balance and reconcile that with its responsibility to the nation, the society, and humanity at large. At all points in time, the direction of a public organization should transcend the personal values of the organizational leadership. As private organizations use codes of ethics and their corporate cultures to govern behaviors, public organizations may as well, use such codes for the political appointees; as well as for the career employees and leaders.

Whatever the ethical perspective adopted by a public organization, it must counter its disdvantages by developing codes of ethics; as well as the enforcement of professional and applied ethics. Applied ethics reflect on moral dilemmas and moral problems in different social contexts or arenas[3]. Applied ethics deal with specific realms of human action and the attempts to determine the criteria for discussing any issues arising within those realms[2]. Applied ethics essentially focus on such domain-specific areas as medicine, business, and engineering[2]. An explanation for the development of applied ethics relates to new moral problems created by the use of technology[3]. An example is the ethical dilemma of keeping the terminally ill alive with medical devices. The ethical delimma becomes; would that be about preserving the person's life or prolonging the person's death?

Professional ethics define and clarify professional works and its typical values; and also embody the rights and obligations that are peculiar to the profession[1]. There are professionally accepted standards of behavior and guiding principles in every profession. The understanding of professional ethics is important because, being a professional practitioner entails the acceptance of certain responsibilities to the public. Although, professional ethics mirror applied ethics; professional ethics emanates from the moral experiences of professionals in their work[3].

General Perspectives of Ethics

The appropriate ethical approach in public organizations requires that public leaders and administrators be cognizant of the consequences of their administrative actions in terms of their impacts on such values as liberty, justice, and human dignity[5]. Three general perspectives of normative ethics are; the Utilitarian approach, Kant's categorical Imperative approach, and the Justice as fairness (distributive justice) approach.

Utilitarian perspectives

The utilitarian perspective to ethics or utilitarianism is built on the premise that ethical choices should be based on their consequences[4]. The concept aims at compelling individuals to consider the potential outcomes of their decisions during the decision-making processes. The nineteeth century philosopher, John Stuar Mill (1806-1873) formalized this perspective of ethics; propounding that the best ethical decisions are those that generate the most advantages than disadvantages; as well as benefiting the largest number of people[4].

This ethical perspective conceptually espouses the greatest good for the greatest number of people. The approach essentially holds that moral behavior should produce the greatest good for the greatest number. Some idealists tend to take this utilitarian perspective that an act is right if it produces the greatest good for the greatest number of people affected by the action; even though it may be harmful to a certain group[6]. Usually, the utilitarian question is; what course of action brings the greatest good for the greatest number of people?

The advantages of this ethical perpective in public organization is that it is easy to understand, frequently used; and above all, compels public orgnizations to examine the potential outcomes of the decisions or public policies. Although, the formulators of public policies and the decision-makers may always reach different conclusions as to the potential outcomes, the arising policy debates are always healthy for the body politic. This focus on potential outcomes also encourages policy makers to think through their decisions; thereby reducing rashness and unreasoned choices[4]. An exemplary application of the utilitarian ethics are the usual actions taken by the medical units in combat situations; during which the physicians usually give top priority to the treatment of soldiers who are most likely to survive their woulds or injuries. Other more complex situations for public organizations could be what programs or services to dispense with; when, for instance, budgets are reduced. Every public department usually believes that it serves important public purpose and good; making it most likely that different conclusions on benefits and outcome consequences would be reached.

Rightly or wrongly, this was the ethical perspective espoused by political administrators in the Harry Truman presidency; in the justification of the nucear bombing of the Japanese cities of Hiroshima and Nagasaki to end the war with Japan during the World War II. These political administrators argued that the benefits of reducing the tremendous loss of American lives in the pacific war theaters outweighed the consequences of destroying these two Japanese cities, including the tremendous loss of Japanese lives.

For the reasons of the high likelihood of reaching conflicting conclusions, some historians have concluded that the nuclear bombing of Japan was unnecessary as the war would still have ended pretty soon without the need to deploy such devastating nuclear arsenal on the two Japanese cities. They also argue that no military or human objective justified such widespread destruction; especially with its continual adverse consequences of cancer afflictions in the two Japanese cities[4]. Some disadvantages of this perspective, therefore, include that it may be difficult to identify or evaluate all the potential consequences as exmplified by the nuclear bombing of Japan; which also triggered off the nuclear arms race. Outcomes can, therefore, have unintended consequences.

Kant's Categorical Imperative Perspectives

In his work, *Groundwork of the Metaphysis of Morals*, German Philosopher Immanuel Kant (1724-1804), espoused a contrasting perpective to utilitarian ethics; and argued that individuals should just do what is morally right regardless of the consequences[4]. This pespective, known as Kant's Categorical Imperative emphasizes the duty and importance of treating humanity as an end; professing that "what is right for one is right for all[4]. Based on this reasoning, such acts as truth telling and helping the poor are universally right; whereas, lying, cheating, and murder are always wrong; whatever the circumstances might be[4]. This is a universalistic approach that is based on the rights of the individuals. It weighs the 'rightness' and 'wrongness' of actions, based on their adherence or violations of some universal moral principles.

From this perspective, it is morally wrong for oil companies to ignore their polutions in African Countries; whereas they quickly clean and pay compensation when they pollute the environment in Western countries. For instance, the giant oil company, Shell BP, had been spilling oil and polluting Ogoniland Nigeria for decades. The decades of spillage had continously polluted the drinking water, fishing creeks, farmlands, and outdoor air of the Ogoni people and the sorrounding communities[8]. Although, these coomunities had been degradated, humiliated, and poisoned by the pollution; yet they continued to drink, bath, wash, and cook with the water, as they had no alternatives. The members of these communities could not, however, fish or farm any longer; as their farms and fishing creeks had been completely destroyed. The pollutions created obvious and immense damages to the communities; leading to widespread hunger and malnutrition, diseases, low living standards, reduced life spans, and mass exodus of people from the communities.

Then, in the later years of the 80s, the Ogoni people, led by the environmental activist, Ken Saro Wiwa began to demand for clean-up and to hold Shell accountable. Rather than clean up the spillage, Shell, it was alleged, connived with the ruling military dictatorship in Nigeria to forcefully occupy and intimate the Ogoni people. During the period of harrassment and intimidation, the ruling military dictorship framed up false charges against the protesting environmentalist. Using a special military tribunal (and not the usual court system), the junta imposed death penalties; and carried out the 1994 extra-judicial hanging of Ken Saro Wiwa and eight other Ogoni leaders.

Then again, in august 2008, there were two devastating oil spillages in the 70,000-residents Bodo town in Ogoniland; which, when put together, were as large as the 10 million gallons 1989 Exxon Valdez disaster in Alaska[9]. Shell not only insisted that the spillage was only 40,000 gallons; it also ignored the pleadings of the local communities to clean-up the spillage. It took a class action suit in a British court by the local communities in 2011 before Shell accepted full liability for the spillage[9].

Then, it took multiple petitions to the United Nations and the special report by the United Nations Environmental Programme (UNEP) for Shell to accept to partake in the general clean-up of decades of oil spillaage and environment degradation; committing only $1 billion[9].

Compare the response of Shell to decades of oil spillages in Ogoniland with its response to the deepwater horizon oil spillage that began on the 20th April, 2010 in the United State's Gulf of Mexico. Shell imeddiately accepted responsibility; mobilized 48,000 persons, 6,500 vessels, used up about 70 million personnel hours[8]. Shell also immediately created a $20 billion trust fund to settle any claims arising from the disaster. The Chief executive Offficer was also fired. By 2011, Shell had paid out $14 billion in claims, advances, and settlements; and had also spent $40 billion in costs associated with clean-up and recovery[8].

This Kant's Categorical Imperative perspective to ethics has the advantage of promoting consistency; is highly motivational, and respects the rights and lives of everyone regardless of gender, race, nationality, or location. The emphasis on duty encourages persistency and consistency as behaviors are "driven by the conviction that certain behaviors are either right or wrong regardless of situation[4]. In public affairs, this perspective is most likely to encourage such transcedent principles as justice, truth, and fairness; while condemning such acts as deception, racism, coercion, and violence. This ethical perspective can therefore, serve as powerful tools for employee motivation; as well as for motivational leadership in the management of public organizations and the conduct of public duties.

Opposing views to the Kant's Categorical Imperative perspective indicate that there must be exception to every universal rule; and that the perspective was unrealistic in the past world, and remains unrealistic in the present world. Other opponents criticize this perspective, indicating that public actors may have warped consciences, and therefore, not trusted on their abilities to concisely demarcate right from wrong. On a bright side, public organizations can control the issue of warped conscience by developing codes for the acceptable moral principles or ethical conducts.

Justice as Fairness Perspective

The American philosopher, John Rawls in the book, *A Theory of Justice,* developed this perspective of justice as fairness. This perspective of ethics focuses on fostering cooperation in societies that are made up of free and equal citizens; while at same time, dealing with the inequalities that exist in societies[4]. John Rawls had rejected the utilitarian ethics, arguing that generating the greatest good for the greatest number would seriously disadvantage certain groups and individuals. Rather than adopting the cost-benefit considerations of the utilitarian ethics; public policies should follow the principles of justice and fairness by building them into the organizing documents and legislation of public organizations. These principles would include: equal opportunities to qualify for offices and jobs; forbidding discrimination based on race, gender, or ethic origin; recognizing existing inequalities; and giving priorities to the poor, handicapped persons, and minority groups[4].

When applied to public organizations, it encourages organizational leaders, not only to be fair, but to exhibit the utmost responsibility of guaranteeing basic rights to all employees; such as equal access to promotion, training, and other benefits; and to help employees with special needs[4]. This distributive justice approach requires that rights must be exercised in a way that is fair to all. It requires that individuals or situations that are similar in those aspects that are relevant to a decision be treated the same way. The justice question is; does this action apply impartially to each employee or organizational unit? For instance, should men and women employees receive equal pay for the same job?

Some advantages of this perspective includes that it nurtures individual freedom; as well as fosters the good of the community. It encourages leaders to treat all subordinates fairly; while showing concerns for the less fortunate members of the community. This perspective can serve as a useful decision-making guide for any public organization as it would enable it marshall out condisely, the rights of employees and the rights of the served public. Under, these principles, everyone should have equal access to the available public-provided healthcare, decent housing, and qualitative education. This perpective is likely to contribute to the shrinkage of the gap between the rich and the poor. In the United States, the concept of special accomodation for individuals with disabilities was based on this perspective.

The perspective has, however, been criticized as only applicable to liberal democratic societies in which the rights of individuals reign supreme. Opponents also contend that it is not applicable to persons living under authoritarian regimes or under monarchies. In addition, critics also argue that the definition of justice and fairness widely vary. An example is the Affirmative action clause in university admissions in the United States. Whereas the Blacks and other minorities perceive the programme as justice towards redressing past discrimination; the Whites consider the programme as the denial of equality of opportunity. Based on the perspective of distributive justice; especially with regard to recognition of existing inequalities, affirmative action program is obviously a pursuit of equality of opportunity, as well as efforts at addressing past inequalities.

Chapter 26

Applications of Values and Ethics in Public Organizations

The key values of governance in any country are usually spelt out in its constitution. In the United States, the constitution (with the amendments) guides and shapes the actions and structure of the government. The values espoused in the United States constitution, are based on the principles that all persons are created equal, and have certain inalienable rights. Other values that have evolved from the constitutional provisions include: equality of the citizenry; the responsiveness and accountability of the government to the governed; the transparency of government actions and services; and the accessibility of all to government programmes and services. These values presume that all are created equal and should be so treated. In its ideal sense, all citizens should be guaranteed the same rights and services from the government. As in most developed democracies, these are the core values under which public organizations are set up. These values define the visions, ethics, and the overall practices in their public organizations.

Core Values of Public Organizations

The core values of a public organization constitute the foundation of its culture; as well as giving a clear understanding of what the organization is about, and where it is headed (the visions). The values and visions of the organization then guide the outlines of the goals and objectives the organization has set forth. The values of an organization are therefore, intertwined with its missions (why it is doing what it is doing); its goals (what it wants to achieve); objectives (what it hopes to accomplish); and its vision (where it is headed)[3]. These values and visions hold the organization firmly together during crisis; as well as during fluctuations in the external environment. For a public organization to avail itself of all the available opportunities, efforts should always be made to align it visions with its core values.

Although, the objectives and rationale of the conventional concepts of public administration have always been the economical, efficient, and coordinated management of public services; the new concepts of public administration has the added rationale of social equity[9]. Social equity as fairness in the delivery of public services; and the right of every citizen to be given equal treatment by the political system, is the new rationale[10]. The social inequalities that reinforce the call for social equity in the American political system have typically been racial, political, and economic. Some countries like India have such distinctive social inequalities as the caste systems.

The pursuit of social equity should be geared toward the enhancement of the political and economic well being of the poor and the minorities. The lack of equity continuously increases the gap between the rich and poor; and usually leads to social and political instabilities. Obviously, the likely result of working from the normative base of social equity is the improvement in social harmony among the diverse groups that make up the citizenry of a nation. The key focus of public organizations in their service deliveries should, therefore, be toward greater equity. Of course, there is the likelihood of resistances from the privileged classes; and the legislatures which they traditionally control.

In the United States, it was the pursuit of these values that evolved into the concepts of common good and equity in public affairs. Obviously, it is the drive towards equity in public affairs that led to the introduction of such programmes as affirmative actions and the social welfare programmes as Medicare, Medicaid, Suplementary Nutrition Assistance Program (SNAP), and the Children's Health Insurance Program (CHIP).

Another value public organizations should bring to bear on

governance is interactions with citizens. It is important for public officers and professionals to meet citizens on their own grounds; as signs that they care and are willing to work with them to respond to their concerns or solve their problems[2]. Public organizations should always cultivate relationships with the citizen-stakeholders before any meaningful policy decision is made. This empowerment of citizens through collaboration is the hallmark of any active and participatory democracy. Public organizations should emphasize this empowerment as encouraging citizens' participation in the public management process is a positive-sum game[2]. With collaboration, citizens can bring their particular knowledge and skills into the delivery and management of public services[2].

Administrative Ethics

Administrative ethics hinge on the moral principles that can be brought to bear on the conduct of public affairs; and on the rights and duties of public officials, as they conduct public duties[9]. Rather than placing emphasis on whose interest public policy serves, the moral issue should be whether the action or policy serves everyone's interest[9].

Two concepts of ethics offer direct challenges to the deployment of administrative ethics in public life. One concept is the ethics of neutrality; which asserts that, public administrators ought to act neutrally by following the decisions and polices of the organization and not their moral principles. This concept requires that public officers carry out the orders of their superiors; and also implement the policies of the public organizations and the government they serve. Essentially, public administrators should be ethically neutral; and not exercise independent moral judgment[9]. The subordinate public administrators are not to act on any moral principles of their own; but are to give effect to whatever principles that are reflected in the orders and policies they are charged with implementing.

While downplaying the fact that subordinate public administrators have discretionary powers, this concept tends to impede the accountability of administrators to citizens. This is because, by reinforcing the illusion that subordinate public administrators do not exercise independent moral judgment, it insulates them from external accountability for the consequence of many of their decisions. This administrative ethic was used in the arguement that those lawyers in George Walker Bush's justice department who advised that water boarding was not torture (a crime in the United States); as well as those operatives who carried out the water boarding of war prisoners at the Guantanamo Bay, Cuba, be shielded from prosecution.

The other concept is that of ethics of structure; which indicates that the organization (and its formal leaders and officers), and not the subordinate administrators should be held responsible for its decisions and policies. Even if the subordinate public administrators may have some scope for independent moral judgment, they cannot be held morally responsible for most of the decisions and policies of government[9]. The concept asserts that the moral responsibility of the subordinate public administrators should extend only to the specific duties and actions of their own office, for which they are legally liable. The proponents of the ethics of structure argue that, although patterns and policies could be condemned, the individual official cannot be morally blamed for it. They further argue that even when the policy of the organization is morally wrong, each individual has done his or her moral duty according to the requirements of office, and therefore, not be held accountable. If these arguments are found acceptable, then guilty subordinate public officials should always be let off the moral hook. Moreover, without some sense of personal responsible, officials may act with less moral care; and citizen may challenge officials with less moral effect.

The ethic of neutrality suppresses independent moral judgment; whereas, the ethic of structure ignores individual moral responsibility in public organizations. Neither of these concepts constitutes an ethic or a morality; as each denies the presuppositions of moral judgment that a person judge or be judged. As administrative ethics require the application of moral principles in the conduct of public affairs and organizations, both the ethics of neutrality and ethics of structure concepts should be rejected.

The applications of moral principles in public affairs require the specification of the rights and duties that public officers should respect when their actions are likely to seriously affect the well-being

160

of individuals or the society at large[12]. Second, it should also specify the conditions which the collective practices and policies should satisfy when they are likely to affect the well-being of individuals or the society[12]. The society should be able to hold the public officials to a higher standard than ordinary citizens; thereby assuring that they would foresee and take into accounts a wider range of the consequences of their actions. Obviously, so long as the welfare of so many is at stake, public officials must make exceptional efforts to anticipate consequence of their actions.

Work Ethics (The Ethics of Hardwork)

The work ethics of any group of people always plays a great role in the development of their society. Work ethic is a cultural norm that places a positive moral value on doing a good job; with the belief that work has an intrinsic value for its own sake[4]. The concept of work ethic has, however, undergone various and contradicting interpretations over the course of human creation and evolution.

In the traditional Judeo-Christian beliefs, work was viewed as a curse devised by God to punish humanity for the disobedience and ingratitude of Adam and Eve[4]. In a similar reasoning, the ancient Greeks also regarded work as a curse[6]. They considered mechanical works as "brutalizing to the mind" and skill works appropriate only for the slaves[4]. Even such classical philosophers like Plato and Aristotle indicated that the purpose for which the majority of men should labour was in order that the elites engage in such pure exercises of the mind like art, philosophy, and politics[11]. The ancient Romans also viewed work as tasks fit for slaves; and that the occupations suitable for a free man were agriculture and business[6]. Even during the medieval periods, work was also still perceived as punishment by God for man's original sin[11]; but a little more acceptable because of its wealth creating potentials.

This negative concept of work changed during the period of the reformation, which was engineered by Martin Luther and John Calvin. Martin Luther taught that people could serve God through their work; and that all callings were of equal spiritual dignity[4]. Similarly, John Calvin taught that all men must work because to work was the will of God[4]. This era became the origin of the "protestant ethics" of hard work. The key elements of the "protestant ethics" of hard work were diligence, punctuality, deferment of gratification, and primacy of work domain[8]. The protestant sects of Christianity spread this concept; but it later assumed a materialistic and individualistic perspective throughout Europe and America. In America, the concept triumphed during the industrial revolution with economists warning that poverty and decay would befall the country if people failed to work hard[7].

The "protestant ethics" of hard work stress personal responsibility; and that compensation and rewards should be based on equity. That is, reward in proportion to contribution. Equity in this regard, is the balance between the inputs an individual brings to a job and the outcomes he or she receives from it[5]. This equity theory postulates that for any kind of reward to have the desired effect, it must be equitable. As the individual incentive programs tend to yield higher productivity in the American work environment; the lesson for the organizational leader is to orient the reward system in the public workplace toward individual incentives.

In this information age, productive work ethics suggest that job satisfaction is enhanced by worker participation in the decision-making processes. People have begun to find self-fulfillment in their work as information age jobs provide opportunities for greater self-expression[4]. The leader's strategic human resource practices should, therefore, be more employee-oriented. The orientation should be that of the encouragement of full employee participation in important matters. Employee participation should be an imperative as it enables organizations maintain high commitment and high performance among employees; and ultimately, organizational effectiveness. The lessons to the organizational leaders from the evolution of the work ethics are the neccesity of work orientation with regards to reward, compensation, motivation, and leadership.

Code of Ethics

As issues of ethics tend to exist in most public decision-making processes and actions, creating ethical dilemmas when right or wrong cannot be clearly identified. As each alternative has a potentially harmful ethical consequence, codes of ethics have assumed greater importance in the conduct of public organizations. Moreover, as neither the administrative ethics nor ethics of structure has been found capable of creating the ethical and moral platforms that would guarantee the ethical accountability of leaders in public organizations; it becomes imperative that each public organization should have a code of ethics.

Establishing a code of ethics is a very important part of leadership; as it can aid the organization in its efforts to provide the open and ethical culture that is conducive for organizational success. The leadership must adopt a code of ethics and a standard of conduct. These ethics and codes of conduct must be constantly communicated to the employees in simple and concise formats. In addition, organizational policies must reflect these values and codes of conduct.

The policies must be clear and concise, and should provide operational and practical guidance to the line managers and department heads; as well as help them deal with pluasible or potential problems[1]. Such potential problems can include discrimination, sexual harassment, conflict of interest, bribery, corruption, illegal gifting or receipt, confidentiality, and political activities; as well as the issues involved in the provision of special accomodations for handicapped persons.

The leadership and employees would be expected to conform to the stated values of the organization; as well as to its code of conducts. There must also be procedures for monitoring adherence to the code ethics. There should be no gap between expectation and behaviour[1]. Other leadership-based strategies for reinforcing an organization's code of ethics include; exemplary ethical and moral leadership by both the senior management and appointed top officials. For the employees, there must be adequate protection for whistleblowers for the valid disclosures of ethical violations or other misconducts. There must also be some mandatory ethics training for employees at the time of employment; and mandatory re-training as either a first reprimand, or as sanctions for minor infractions. Above all, and as proactive steps, documented evidence of ethical behaviors should also be one of the major criteria for promotions to management positions.

Chapter 27

Corruption: Ethical Deviance in Public Organizations

Corruption is the intentional deviation from established standards, principles, policies, regulations, codes of conduct, or ethics codes for the purpose of personal gain and selfish purposes. Corruption in public organizations can simply be defined as the inappropriate use of public office for private gain[5]. Corruption can also be described as the unauthorized use of public office for private gain. Corruption can take on many forms; including, bribery, nepotism, misappropriation of funds; and theft of time, kickbacks, extortion, spoils, and conflicts of interest.

Corruption undermines the economic rights of the citizens. When contracts are illegally awarded by means of bribes, the public's right to have purchases made in most efficient and least costly fashion is undermined. Such corruption makes a mockery of economic considerations and development. Corruption, therefore, leads to misallocation of resources, disrupts economic development, and distorts public policies[1]. Corruption also slows down economic development, crowds out productive investment, raises the cost of business, and reduces the products of public projects[2].

The Beginning and Continum of Corruption

Corruption is the moral decay which commonly arises from failures of individuals and organizations to live up to moral standards[5]. Corruption in public organizations, sometimes, stems from the emulation by subordinates of the illegal behaviors of the leadership. Some public officers have this inexplicable feeling of some sort of entitlement. They rationalize stealing because of the amount of work they do for the little amount of compensation they receive. In other words, some believe it is a perk for working as an employee of the government.

Once that feeling of entitlement sets in, corruption has a chance to take hold. Under this entitlement feeling, the use of public property for personal functions is not only accepted, but usually condoned. Everything from inappropriate personal use of public property, to the performance of personal works on government time, are all too common occurrences. In essence, corruption in most public organizations can range from such small-scale issues as looking the other way when someone takes office supplies, to large-scale crimes such as steering a contract towards a particular bidder.

Corruption is impairment of integrity, virtue, or moral principle; and at its root, corruption is a departure of ethical behavior. Although, the root cuase of corruption is deviance from ethical behaviour, an analysis of what leads a public organization or an individual to become corrupt suggests a continuum[6].

The continum of corruption can be illumerated as follows:
(i)   Phase one, " indifference toward integrity",
(ii)   Phase two, " negligence of obvious ethical problems",
(iii)   Phase, "hypocrisy and fear dominant in the corruption culture," and
(iv)   Phase four, "survival of the fittest"[6].

Obviously, as small unethical acts occur along each phase of the continuum, it is up to the leadership of the organization to stop the corruption, or allow it to flourish. Even as the root of corruption can be found in the actions of individuals, the organizations ought to control the situations in which these individual actions take place. A public organization loses its moral and legislated ability to perform its function when public accountability no longer exists. This same understanding is also applicable to a corrupt public official. The ethical and appropriate organizational response to the initial infraction is the key to either stopping the behavior entirely or healing a very sick organization[3].

Curbing Corruption

Since the creation of the professional civil service in the1870s, certain processes have, over the following decades, been used to monitor and weed out corruption within public administration. Such reform management movements as scientific management, which was initiated by Frederick Winslow Taylor, was put in place in about 1910; with the hopes of further displacing waste, abuse, and corruption from public administration in the United States. In more recent times, the use of monitoring and law enforcement tools have been utilized; and has in some organizations, been combined with decentralization and deregulation.

The main issue with corruption becomes how the organization responds[3]. The problem with the organizational response is, sometimes, rooted in such group pathologies as "groupthinking"[4]. "Group thinking" is used to describe groups that put consensus and unanimous agreements ahead of reasoned problem solving solutions[4]. As groups suffering from this malaise always tend to be close-minded, and tend not to consider important moral issues or all alternatives, such groups tend to make unethical decisions[4]. Under this dispensation, partakers develop a sense of invulnerability; rationalizating their actions and ignoring ethical consequences as they assume authorities of responsibility. Usually, pressure is put on dissenting ones to go along with the prevailing actions of the group[4].

Organizational leaders are usually guilty of ignoring or not knowing the importance of the warning signs. As corruption usually starts with relatively small unethical acts, and then grows to whatever level the leadership allows; leaders are both the causes of and the solutions to corruption. The strategic leader should be able to recognize the red flags that appear before the corruption begins to occur.

Chapter 28

Ethical Leadership in Public Organizations

Leaders of public organizations watch over institutions that embody important public ideals; they therefore, bear a special responsibility to maintain the intergrity of such institutions[3]. As such, it is unquestionably necessary for these leaders to be transparent and value-oriented; and to develop ethical perspectives to leadership[2]. Ethical issues are values that directly relate to beliefs concerning what is right and proper, motivating a sense of moral duty, as opposed to what is simply correct or effective. Ethical leaders should not only be concerned with their own ethical values, but also on how to convey such to others; and thus be able to influence them toward working for common goals and aspirations.

As power is the potential ability to influence the behavior of others, it represents the resources with which a leader can effect changes in employees' behaviors. In any public organization, leadership should not only be responsible, but should also relate to the moral and ethical factors created and agreed upon by the society[8]. Public organizations should, therefore, be eager to develop and nurture the leadership that will not only create quality service, but will also create long-term values that would reflect the required ethical values for the stakeholders[2].

There is a core difference between the exercise of power and leadership. Power is exercised when the power wielder, acting for their own goals, use the avialble resources to influence others[3]. Under the exercise of power, it does not matter whether or not the purpose of the wielders is at variance with the purpose of the respondents. Leadership on the other hand, is exercised when individuals with certain motives and purposes mobilize others and resources to arouse, engage, and satisfy the motives of the followers[3]. The purpose power still very much remains to create a linkage between one's will, and the purpose of others; through reasoning and cooperation. Leadership in public organizations should not be viewed as positions, but rather as an activity defined by the type of service the leader offers. An individual should, therefore, be considered a leader if and only the individual embarks on the appropriate and ethical leadership activities.

A Power-based or Ethics-based Leadership?

The approach to leadership in public organizations can either be power-based or ethics-based. The power-based approach of leadership essentially tends to assume that the primary source of wisdom is the leader or that knowledge is for the benefit of the leader[9]. Generally, the reaction to the power-base approach can be in the form of commitment to the leader's point of view and instructions, or opposition to such. For instance, legitimate power tends to demand compliance by obeying orders and carrying out instructions whether or not the individual shares the view. Such power as coercive power; which gives the leaders authority to punish or withdraw privileges, sometimes leads subordinates to avoid carrying out instructions or to total resistance.

Ethics-based approach to leadership assumes that the leader is not likely to have all the wisdom; and that the followers either have important contribution to make or may even have all the facts and knowledge[9]. In ethics-based leadership, the leader is expected, not only to display high level of ethics, but also be perceived as doing so. It is most understandable that power alone, without moral purpose and reasoned values will not be satisfactory toward the creation of effective and creative ethical leadership[3]. As earlier stated, this ethical approach to leadership requires that public administrators take cognizant of the consequences of administrative action in terms of its impact on such values as; liberty, justice, and human dignity[6].

Although, the leadership of public organizations can involve the exercise of power, such power must be used appropriately; as well as reflecting larger values and purposes[3]. For the reasons of the difficulty in determining the appropriateness of power, its use must be ethical and reflective of moral standards, norms, and values. Moreover, as the exercice of power in public organizations can have influence and impacts on the meaning of law, justice, and governance; ensuring the legitimacy and ethicality of its use is of profound importance.

The Ethical Triangle for Public Leadership

There are ethical factors that are inherent in ethics-based leadership. These ethical factors can be analyzed from perpectives of cognitive and virtues ethics. In cognitive ethics, decisions are hinged on the deployment of the applicable rules, and the expected results[9]. Virtue ethics are anchored on moral reasoning and judgment[9]. Some degree of interdependence and complementarities exist between cognitive and virtue ethics; resulting to an ethical triangle.

This ethical triangle, which results from this relationship, serves to emphasize that virtue is insufficient without cognition; just as cognition is insufficient without virtue[9]. The apexes of this equilateral triangle are: greatest good, justice, and integrity; with all three required to be supporting and reinforcing[9]. The "greatest good" (utilitarian) apex holds that moral behavior should produce the greatest good for the greatest number[5]. This utilitarian concept is pivoted on the premise that ethical choices should be made on the basis of their consequences[5]. The concept postulates that the best decisions are those that generate the most benefits in comparison to their harmfulness; and should also benefit the largest number[5]. This apex indicates that an act is right if it produces the greatest good for the greatest number of people affected by the action[5]. The justice apex demands that rights be exercised in a way that is fair to all. The integrity apex postulates that personal and public actions must be laden with integrity.

Although, the outcomes from decisions made with consideration to the ethical triangle will not always be the same, the concept has more to do with the process than outcome[9]. For a leader in a public organization, acting within the parameters of the ethical triangle will limit the potentialities of unethical decisions[9]. Moreover, since ethical conflicts and delimmas are inherent in decision-making, moral criteria must be integrated into the process[1].

The use of the ethical triangle should not, however, always assume high measure of absoluteness that transcends time and culture; ethical triangle should rather constitute a good guide. For ethical public organizations that desire to operate under the concept of ethical triangle, the leadership should not only insist that decisions be moral; but must also describe the underlying logic and process under which decisions should be made. In essence, the ethical triangle developed by a public organization should create the guide for the best ethical perspectives for any issues that create ethical concerns. The issues should be weighed in the ethical balance constituting of all the three apexes of this equilateral triangle. This is necessary as tilting actions in favor of any of the apexes would cause the triangle to lose its equilateralism; leading to the perceptions of ethics becoming unbalanced and skewed, and the ethicality of outcomes suspect and debatable.

Obviously, ethical leaders who lead by example help to foster the healthy ethical dispositions that are characterized by transparency, trust, integrity, and high moral standards[4]. The ethical orientation of leadership must also extend to relationships with followers and associates; focusing on such worthy objectives as high morality, transparency, openness, and trustworthiness. For instance, as the strength of servant leadership lies on concern for others, simplicity, and moral sensitivity within the organization[5]; there is a greater tendency for the ethic-based approach in the servant leadership model. As transformational leaders hold morality and pragmatism to a high level; and their reasoning based on morality[5]; as often displayed and perceived in the behaviors of the leaders and their followers; ethical-based approach is also likely with this leadership model

As ethical leaders are expected to transform lives and organizations, inspirations alone may not be enough; effective and moral implementation of policies is necessary for the development of the capacity for creating and maintaining the ethical system[7]. Public leadership should therefore, be defined by the type of service the leader offers; as adjudged through the ethical triangle.

Chapter 29

Strategies for Optimizing Your Leadership Skills

(A)   Developing and Optimizing your transformational leadership Skills

For your employees/subordinates

- Always create clear, compelling, and energizing visions that could serve as the unifying focal point of efforts.
- Always inspire and share your visions with your employees/subordinates; empowering them toward achieving the visions.
- Always show your employees/subordinates how their roles are significant within the context of the larger operation.
- Always show appreciation and consideration for your employees/subordinates.
- Focus on arousing the consciousness of your employees/subordinates by appealing to such higher ideals and moral values as; liberty, justice, equality, peace, and humanitarianism.
- Emphasize on such higher order needs of your employees/subordinates such as esteem, competency, self-fulfillment, and self-actualization.
- Always strive to build an empowered dynamic culture, in which employees/subordinates will always have high expectations placed upon them.
- Always strive to create strength when there seems to be weakness; and courage when there seems to be fear.
- Emphasize the personal development and empowerment of your employees/ subordinates by always providing the

necessary resources for the development and achievement of their personal potentials.

- Always trust your employees/subordinates; so as to earn their trusts in return.
- Provide coaching and mentorship on an individual basis.
- Always strive to create and encourage new learning opportunities for your employees/subordinates.
- Always demonstrate concern for your employees/subordinates by extending your efforts toward engaging, motivating, and encouraging employees to adapt to specific goals and objectives of the organization in a manner that ensures quality improvement, not just for the organization, but also for the individual as well.

For Your Self

- Always discourage "personality worshipping" and any tendencies of "personalized idolization".
- Do not, for the sake of promoting your own interest, downplay the contributions of the employees/subordinates.
- Do not encourage your employees/subordinates to become increasing more dependent on you.
- Do not encourage your rise as a 'cult leader' by trying to change the organization to fit your image, rather than fit organizational goals.
- Discourage leader-centricism, in which the direction of the group is determined and focused on you; whereas other individual's efforts are unaccounted and unrecognized.

For the Organization

- Always make conscious efforts to increase morality levels in your organization and among your employees/subordinates.
- Always focus the organization on such terminal values as; liberty, equality, and justice; as they mobilize and energize your employees/subordinates by creating the agenda for actions; as well as appealing to larger audiences.
- Engage your employees/subordinates in such a manner as to raise them to higher levels of morality and motivation;

motivating them to transcend their own interests for the sake of the department or organization.

- Encourage innovation and creativity in your organization.
- Emphasis on the moral element of leadership in the organization.
- Always strive to improve the morale within the organization.
- Emphasize moral character and ethical behavior in organizational policies.
- Always be motivated from a sense of mission for creating self-survivalist measures to internal and external challenges.
- The success of the organization should always be made to relate to the growth and development of the individual employees.
- Always focus toward the empowerment of the people for the purposes of building commitment toward organizational goals
- Always create a sense of mission and purpose, as it helps recreate and strengthen the organization by enhancing its ability to survive challenging external environments.
- Always look at the big picture by focusing on breaking down the strategic steps in such a manner that will ensure clear vision and ther completion of the tasks at hand.

(B)   Developing and Optimizing your servant leadership Skills

Let the motives for your service be stewardship, obligation, partnership, and elevating purpose. Stewardship entails acting serving, protecting, and nurturing your followers or subordinates.

For your followers/colleagues
- Your motivation should only be the desire to serve. You should always see leadership as an opportunity to serve others.
- Your primary focus should be on your followers/colleagues; with the achievement of organizational objectives as a subordinate outcome.
- Always strive to build up the spiritual generative culture in which followers/colleagues emphasize their own personal growth; and the growth of other members and the organization.
- Always show concern for the overall welfare of group members rather than self-comfort.
- Always strive to move followers beyond their self-interests for the good of the group.
- Always help your followers/colleagues to grow and develop as productive members of society.
- Always allow followers/colleagues to assume leadership roles when conditions warrant.
- Discourage any potential for manipulations.
- Remember you only function as agents of your followers/colleagues who have entrusted you with duties and opportunities for a limited time.

For Yourself
- Always be selfless, simplistic, and morally sensitive to stewardship; valuing and developing people; building communal interests; and providing leadership and sharing leadership.

- Anchor your leadership philosophy on putting the needs of your subordinates before your own needs.
- Believe that by sharing your leadership in partnership with subordinates you can effectively function as a trustee.
- Remember your success will be measured in terms of the extent your followers/colleagues achieve their self-actualization; and you would be judged by what happens in their lives.
- Always recognize the needs of employees/colleagues in the context of operational success of the organization. If employees/colleagues are happy in their work life, there is an excellent possibility that the organization itself will thrive.
- Focus on developing good relationships with your followers/colleagues.
- Always place the good of your followers/colleagues ahead of your self-interest; placing emphasis on serving them as opposed to the reverse.
- Always lead by example; and always seek to satisfy the needs of your followers/colleagues, who happen to be your master.
- Always remember your followers/colleagues have equal rights to vision, respect, and information; as you are supposed to know no better than them.
- Your followers/colleagues are your partners; you are nothing but a trustee; and the growth and development of the individual are the goals.
- Always show appreciation and consideration for your followers/colleagues.
- Your focus should also be on people; with the primary emphasis on service, rather than organizational results.
- You should always be eager to provide resources and support to followers/colleagues without expectation of acknowledgement.
- You should always demonstrate concern for the welfare and development of your followers/colleagues by influencing them through personal development and empowerment.

175

- Your goal should always include the incorporation and promotion of moral sensitivity.

For the Organization
- You must share the belief that the best way to achieve organizational goals would be through the development of the potential of the employees.
- Always stay focused on achieving results in line with the organization's values and integrity.
- Always be engaged with protecting and nurturing the employees and the organization; whereas making sure that they collectively serve the common good.
- Be passionate about creating and maintaining an impermeable culture of trust, consistency, and reliability.
- Decision-making should always involve most members of the organization, as that will usually result to consensus.
- Under the generative spiritual culture, you should always foster harmony, collaboration, and cooperation.
- Encourage innovation and creativity.
- Always emphasize the moral element of leadership.
- Always strive to improve the morale within the organization.
- Emphasize moral character and ethical behavior.
- Your leadership paradigm should always articulate principles that shape individual and organizational behaviors.
- With the foresight and commitment to the people, develop a long-term approach to life and work; especially as it relates to the systematic processes of implementing positive changes in society; using the tools available in your organization.

BIBLIOGRAPHICAL NOTES

Chapter 1
Forms and Nature of Public Organizations
1. Denhardt, R. B., Denhardt, J.V. & Aristigueta, M.P. (2008). *Managing human behavior in public & nonprofit organizations*. Thousand Oaks, CA: Sage.
2. Dooley, K.J. (1997). A complex Adaptive Systems Model of Organizational Change. Nonlinear Dynamics, *Psychology, and Life Sciences, Vol.* 1 (1).
3. Johnson, C.E. (2005). *Meeting the Ethical Challenges of Leadership: Casting light or shadow*. Thousand Oaks, CA: Sage.
4. Kreitner & Kinicki (2004). *Organizational behavior.* New York: McGraw-Hill.
5. Lulofs, R.S. & Cahn, D.D. (2000). *Conflict from Theory to Action.*Boston: Allyn & Bacon.
6. Selznick, P. In Shafritz, J.M. & Ott, J.S. (2001). *Classics of Organizational Theory.* .New York: Harcourt College Publishers.
7. Shafritz, J.M. & Ott, J.S. (2001). Classics of Organizational Theory.New York: Harcourt College Publishers.
8. Shafritz, J.M., Russell, E.W. & Borick, C.P. (2007). *Introducing Public Administration.*5[th]Ed.New York: Pearson-Longman.

Chapter 2
Public Organizations as Complex Adaptive Systems
1. Brown, D. (1999) Reading, Writing and Regime Type: Democracy's impact on Primary School Enrollment. Political Research Quarterly, Volume 52, pp. 681-707.
2. Chan, Serena (2001). ESD.83 research Seminar in Engineering Systems. Oct 31, 2001- November 6, 2001. Www. MIT.edu/esd83.
3. Dooley, K.J. (1997). A complex Adaptive Systems Model of Organizational Change. Nonlinear Dynamics, Psychology, and Life Sciences, Vol. 1 (1).
4. Duin, A. H., & Baer, L. L. (2010). Shared leadership for a green, global, and Google world. Planning for Higher Education, 39(1), 30-38.
5. Eidelson, R. J. (1997). Complex Adaptive Systems in Behavioral and Social Sciences. Review of General Psychology, vol. 1 (1), 47-71.
6. Fahey, L. & Narayanan, V. K. (1986). Macro environmental analysis for strategic Management. St Paul, MN: West.
7. Olson, E, E, & Eoyang, G.H. (2001). *Facilitating Organization Change: Lessons from Complexity Science.*San Francisco: Jossey-Bass-Pfeiffer.
8. Pascale, R.T., Millemann, M. &Gioja, L. (2000). Surfing the Edge of Chaos: The Laws of Nature and the New Laws of Business. New York: Crown Business.
9. Saadat, Payam (2015). A complex Adaptive System perspective to appreciation Inquiry: A theoretical Analysis. Leadership & Organizational Management Journal, Vol. 2015 (2), 127-142.
10. Schneider, M., & Somers, M. (2006). Organizations as complex adaptive systems: Implications of complexity theory for leadership research. The Leadership Quarterly, 17(4), 351-365.
11. Sherman, H. & Schultz, R. (1998).Open Boundaries. New York: Perseus Books.
12. Tower, D. (2002). Creating the Complex Adaptive organization: A primer on Complex Adaptive Systems.*OD Practitioner*, Volume *34* (3).
13. Watkins. & Cooperrider, D. (2000). Appreciative Inquiry: A Transformative Paradigm. Journal of the Organizational Development Network, Vol.32 (1).

Chapter 3
Theories of Organizational Change
1. Abrahamson, E. (2000). Change without Pain. *Harvard Business Review.* (July/August), pp.75-79.

2. Bechtold, B.L. (1997). Chaos Theory as a Model for Strategy Development. *Empowerment in Organizations*. Vol. 5 (4). Pp.193-202.
3. Buchanan, D., Fitzgerald, L, Ketley, D., Gollop, R.Jones, J.Lamont, S.S., Neath, A. &Whitby, E. (2005).No Going Back: A Review of the Literature on Sustaining Organizational Change. *International Journal of Management Reviews,* Vol. 7 (3). Pp.189-205.
4. Burnes, B. (2004). Kurt Lewin and Complexity Theories: Back to the Future? *Journal of Change Management. Vol, 4* (4). P.311.
5. Collins, B. (1998). *Organizational Change*. London: Routledge.
6. Cuthbertson, J. (2005). Business across Cultures. *Business Book Review*.Vol.22 (19).
7. Dawson, C. (1994). *Organizational Change: Processual Approach*, London: Paul Chapman Publishing.
8. Frederick, W.C. (1998). Creatures, corporations, communities, choas, and complexity: a Neurological view of the Corporate Social Role. *Business and Society*, 37(4). pp.358-376.
9. Gilley, A., McMillian, H. S., & Gilley, J. W., (2009). Organizational change and characteristics of leadership effectiveness. *Journal of Leadership and Organizational studies, 16* (1).
10. Huczynsski, A & Buchanan.(2001).Organizational Behavior ,4th Ed.Harloew:Ft/Prentice – Hall
11. Kreitner, R. & Kinicki, A. (2004). *Organizational behavior.* New York: McGraw-Hill.
12. Kuhn, T.S. (1970). *The Structure of Scientific Revolutions*.2nd Ed.Chicago: University of Chicago Press.
13. Matlin, M.W. & Stang, D.J. (1978). *Pollyanna Principle*.Cambridge, MA: Schenkman.
14. Moran, J.W. & Avergun, A. (1997). Creating Lasting Change. The TQM Magazine, 9(2), 146-157.
15. Peters, T. & Waterman, R.H. (1982). *.In Search of Excellence: Lessons from America's Best-Run Companies*. London: Harper and Row.
16. Watson, T.J. (1997). *In Search of Management.* London: Thompson International.
17. Weick, K.E. & Sutcliffe, K.M. (2001). *Managing the unexpected-Assuring High Performance in an Age of Complexity*. San Francisco, CA: Jossey-Bass.

Chapter 4
Models for Implementing Changes in Public Organizations

1. Berman, E.M., Bowman, J.S; West, J.P. & Van Wart, M. (2001). *Human Resource Management in Public Service: Paradoxes, Processes, and Problems.* Sage Publications: Thousand Oaks: CA.
2. Koteen, J. ((1997). *Strategic Management in Public and Nonprofit Organizations: Managing Public Concerns in an Era of Limits.* Westport; Connecticut: Praeger.
3. Kotter, J.P. (1995). Leading Change: Why transformation Efforts Fail. Harvard Business Review, Vol.73 (2), 59-67.
4. Kreitner, R. & Kinicki, A. (2004). *Organizational behavior.* New York: McGraw-Hill.
5. Meynell, F. (2005). A second-order approach to evaluating and facilitating organizational change. *Action Research* 3:2, 211-231.
6. Tichy, N.M. & Devanna, M.A. (1986). *The Transformational Leader*. New York: John Wiley.

Chapter 5
Success Factors for Managing Change in Public Organizations

1. Ahn, M. J; Adamson, J. A. & Dornbusch, D. (2004). From leaders to leadership: Managing change. *The Journal of Leadership and Organizational Studies*, 10 (4).

2. Buchanan.D, Fitzgerald, L, Ketley, D., Gollop, R.Jones, J.Lamont, S.S., Neath, A. &Whitby, E. (2005). No Going Back: A Review of the Literature on Sustaining Organizational Change. International Journal o Management Reviews, Vol. 7 (3). pp.189-205.
3. Cuthbertson, J. (2005). Business across Cultures. *Business Book Review*.Vol.22 (19).
3a. David & Michael (2005). In Yazeen, Z. & Okour, A. (2012). Managing Organizational change: Decision's maker perceptions in the UAE Manufacturing industry. *International Journal of Research Studies in Management*, Vol. 1 (1), 97-108.
3b. Goold, M., & Campbell, A. (2002). Designing effective organizations: How to create structured networks. San Francisco, CA: Jossey-Bass.
3c. Hebda, J. M., Vojak, B. A., Griffin, A., & Price, R. L. (2007). Motivating Technical visionaries in large American companies. IEEE Transactions on Engineering Management, 54(3), 433-444.
3d. Kanter, R. M. (2003). Leadership for change: Enduring skills for change masters. Boston, MA: Harvard Business Review.
4. Kotter, J.P. (2012). Leading Change. Boston, MA: Harvard Business Review Press.
5. Mackenzie, M.L. (2007). Leadership in the Information Age: A culture of continual Change. *Bulletin of the American society for information science and Technology,* Volume 33(4).
6. Reilly, E. (2007). Adaptability: Key to Survival. *T + D,* Vol.61 (1). P.16.
7. Rousseau, D.M. (1995). *Psychological Constructs in Organizations: Understanding Written and Unwritten Agreements*. Thousand Oaks, CA: Sage.
8. Trice, H.M. & Beyer, J.M. (1986). Cultural Leadership in Organizations. *Organizational Science*, Volume *2*, pp.149-169.
9. Upshur-Myles, C.C. (2007).What followers want from Leaders: Capitalizing on Diversity. *Nonprofit World,* Vol.25 (5).
10. Wheatley, M.J. (1999). *Leadership and the new Science: discovering order in a chaotic World.* San Francisco: Berrett-Kocher publishers.

Chapter 6
Models for Employee Motivation.

1. Aldefer, C. (1972). *Existence, Relatedness, and Growth.* New York: Free Press.
2. Arnolds, C.A. & Bashoff, C. (2002). Compensation, Esteem Valence and Job Performance: An Empirical Assessment of Alderfer's ERG Theory. *International Journal of Human Resource Management.* Volume *13*(4), 697-719.
3. Berman, E.M., Bowman, J.S; West, J.P. & Van Wart, M. (2001). *Human Resource Management in Public Service: Paradoxes, Processes, and Problems.* Sage Publications: Thousand Oaks: CA.
4. Bluen, S.D.; Barling, J. & Burns, W. (1990). Predicting Sales Performance, Job Satisfaction, and Depression by Using the Achievement Strivings and Impatience-Irritability Dimensions of Type A Behavior. *Journal of Applied Psychology*, April Edition, pp.212-216.
5. Denhardt, R. B., Denhardt, J.V. & Aristigueta, M.P. (2008). *Managing human behavior in public & nonprofit organizations*. Thousand Oaks, CA: Sage.
6. Herzberg, F. (1966). *Work and Nature of Man.*Cleveland, OH: World.
7. Jones, G.R, George, J.M. & Hill, C.W. (2000). *Contemporary Management.*2nd Ed.New York: The McGraw-Hill Companies.
8. Kreitner & Kinicki, 2004, p. 260). Kreitner, R. & Kinicki, A. (2004). *Organizational behavior.* New York: McGraw-Hill.
9. Maslow, A. (1943). A theory of Human Motivation. *Psychological Review*. Vol.*50*, 370-396.
10. McClelland, D. (1985). *Human Motivation.*Glenview, IL: Scott, Foresman.
11. McShane, S.L. & Von Glinov, M. A. (2005). *Organizational behavior*. New York: The McGraw-Hill.

179

12. Shafritz, J.M., Russell, E.W. & Borick, C.P. (2007). *Introducing Public Administration.*5thEd.New York: Pearson-Longman.
13. Vroom, V. (1964). *Work and Motivation.* New York: John Wiley.

Chapter 7
The Classical Theories of Leadership

1. Bass, B.M. (1990). From Transactional to Transformational Leadership: Learning to Share the Vision. *Organization Dynamics,* pp.1819-1831.
2. Denhardt, R. B., Denhardt, J.V. & Aristigueta, M.P. (2008). *Managing human behavior in public & nonprofit organizations.* Thousand Oaks, CA: Sage.
3. Fiedler, F.E. (1977). *Job Engineering For Effective Leadership: A New Approach. Management Review.* September Edition, p.29.
4. Hodgetts, R.M., Luthans, F. & Doh, J.P. (2005). *International management: Culture, strategy, and behavior,* 6th Ed.
5. Hersey, P. & Blanchard, K.H. (1988). *Management of organizational behavior: utilizing human resources.* 5th Edition. Eaglewood Cliffs, New Jersey: Prentice -Hall.
6. House, R.J. (1971). A Path-Goal theory of leader effectiveness. *Administrative Science Quarterly, September Edition,* pp.321-338.
7. House, R.J. & Mitchell, T.R. (1974) Path-Goal Theory of Leadership. *Journal of Contemporary Business,* Autumn Edition, pp.81-97.
8. Kreitner, R. & Kinicki, A. (2004). *Organizational behavior.* New York: McGraw-Hill.
9. McShane, S.L. & Von Glinov, M. A. (2005). *Organizational behavior.* New York: The McGraw-Hill.
10. Stogdill, R.M. (1974). *Handbook of Leadership.* New York: Free Press.
11. Van Wart, M. & Dicke, L.A. (2008). *Administrative leadership in the public sector.* Armonk, NY: M.E.Sharpe.

Chapter 8
The New Perspectives of Leadership

1. Ardichvili, A. & Kuchinke, P (2002). Leadership Styles and Cultural Values among Managers and Subordinates: Comparative Study of Four countries of the Former Soviet Union, Germany and the U.S.Human Resource Development International, 5(1).
2. Avolio, B.J. Bass, B. M. & Jung, D.I. (1999). Re-examining the components of transformational and transactional Leadership using the multifactor leadership questionnaire. *Journal of occupational and Organizational Psychology.*Volume*17* (4).
3. Bardwick, J.M. (1996). *Peacetime management and wartime leadership.* In Hessekbein, F; Goldsmith, M; & Beckhard, R.*The leader of the future.* San Francisco, CA: Jossey-Bass.
4. Bass, B.M. (1985). *Leadership and performance beyond expectations.* New York, NY: Free Press.
5. Bass, B.M. & Avolio, B.J. (1994). *Improving Organizational Effectiveness through Transformational Leadership.* Thousand Oaks, CA: Sage.
6. Burns, J.M. (1978). *Leadership.* New York: Harper & Row.
7. Cuilla, J. B. (2004). *Ethics, the heart of leadership.* Westport, CT: Praeger Publishers.
8. Clapp-Smith, R., Vogelgesang, G.R; & Avey, J.B. (2009). Authentic Leadership and Positive Psychological Capital: The Mediating role of trust at Group level of Analysis. *Journal of Leadership & Organizational Studies,* Volume *15*(3), Pp.227-240.
9. Convey, S.R. (1991). *Principle-Centered Leadership.* New York: Summit Books.
10. Daft, R (1995). Understanding Management. New York: The Dryden Press.
11. Denhardt, R. B., Denhardt, J.V. & Aristigueta, M.P. (2008). *Managing human behavior in public & nonprofit organizations.* Thousand Oaks, CA: Sage.

12. Gardner, W.L., Avolio, B.J; Luthans, F.May, D.R. & Walumbwa, F. (2005). Can you see the real me? A self-based model of authentic Leader and Follower development. *Leadership Quarterly*, Volume *16*, 343-372.
13. Hellriegel, D. & Slocum, J.W. (2007). *Organizational Behavior*. Mason, OH: Thomson/South-Western.
14. Johnson, C.E. (2005). Meeting the Ethical Challenges of Leadership: Casting light or shadow. Thousand Oaks, CA: Sage.
15. Kernis, M.H. (2003). Toward Conceptualization of Optimal Self-Esteem. *Psychological Inquiry*, Vol. 14, 1-26.
16. Kotter, J. (1990). *A force for Change.How Leadership Differs from Management*. New York: Guilford Press.
17. Larson, C.E. & LaFasto, F.M. (1989).*Teamwork.* Newbury Park, CA: Sage.
18. Laub, J.A. (1999). *Assessing the servant organization. Development of the servant Organizational Leadership Assessment (SOLA) instrument*. Florida Atlantic University Dissertation.
19. Meindl, J. R., Ehrlich, S. B., & Dukerich, J. M. (1985). The romance of leadership. *Administrative Science Quarterly, vol. 30, 78-102.*
20. Rost, J. (1993). Leadership in the New Millennium. *Journal of Leadership Studies*, Vol. *1*, .92-110.
21. Schuster, J. (1994). Transforming your leadership style. *Association Management*, Volume *46* (1), pp. L39-L43.
22. Smith, B. N., Montagno, R. V., & Kuzmenko, T. N. (2004). Transformational and servant leadership: Content and contextual comparisons. *Journal of Leadership and Organizational Studies,* 10 (4), 81-91.
23. Stone, A.G., Russell, R.F & Patterson, K. (2003). *Transformational Versus Servant Leadership-A difference in Leader Focus*. Paper presented at the servant Leadership Roundtable at Regent University, Virginia Beach, VA, on October, 16, 2003.
24. Trevion, L.K., Brown, M. & Hartman, L.P. (2003). A qualitative investigation of perceived Executive Ethical Leadership: Perceptions from Inside and Outside the Executive Suite. *Human Relations.* Vol. *56*(1), 5-28.
25. Trice, H.M. & Beyer, J.M. (1986). Cultural Leadership in Organizations. *Organizational Science*, Volume *2*, pp.149-169.
26. Trottier, T, Van Wart, M., & Wang, X. (2008). Examining the Nature and Significance of Leadership in Government Organizations. *Public Administration Review*, Vol. *68* (2), 319-334.
27. Tucker, B.A. & Russell, R.F. (2004). The Influence of the Transformational Leader. *Journal of Leadership and Organizational Studies,* Vol. 10(4).
28. Walumbwa, F.O., Avolio, B.J., Gardner, W.L; Wernsing, T.S. & Peterson, S.J. (2008). Authentic Leadership: Development and Analysis of a multidimensional theory-based measure. *Journal of management,* Vol. *34*, 89-126.
29. Whetstone, J.T. (2002). Personalism and moral leadership: The servant leader with a transforming. Business Ethics: A European Review, Vol. *11*(4), 385-392.

Chapter 9
Models for Normative Leadership

1. Bass, B.M. (1985). *Leadership and performance beyond expectations*. New York, NY: Free Press.
2. Bass, B.M. & Avolio, B.J. (1994). *Improving Organizational Effectiveness through Transformational Leadership*. Thousand Oaks, CA: Sage.
3. Bass, B., & Steidlmeier, P. (2004). *Ethics, character, and authentic transformational leadership behavior*. In J. Ciulla (Ed.). *Ethics, the heart of leadership*. Westport, CT: Praeger.

181

4.   Bateman, M. a. (2007). Leading & Collaborating in a Competitive World (7th Ed.). Irvin: Magraw-Hill.
5.   Cassel, J., & Holt, T. (2008, October). The Servant Leader. *American School Board Journal*, volume *196*(10), 34-35.
6.   Cuilla, J. B. (2004). *Ethics, the heart of leadership.* Westport, CT: Praeger Publishers.
7.   Clawson, A. (2006). *Level Three Leadership: Getting Below the Surface*. 3rd Ed.Upper Saddle River, NJ: Pearson/Prentice Hall.
8.   Denhardt, R. B., Denhardt, J.V. & Aristigueta, M.P. (2008). *Managing human behavior in public & nonprofit organizations*. Thousand Oaks, CA: Sage.
9.   DiStefano, J. (1995) *Tracing the Vision and Impact of Robert K.Greenleaf*. In Spears L. (Ed.) Reflections on Leadership. New York: John Wiley & Sons.
10.   Felfe, J. & Schyns, B. (2004). Is similarity in Leadership related to organizational outcomes? The case of transformational Leadership. *Journal of Leadership & Organizational studies*, vol. 10(4).
11.   Graham, J.W. (1991).Servant leadership in Organizations: Inspirational and moral. *Leadership Quarterly*, Vol. *2*(2), 105-119.
12.   Greenleaf, R. K. (1977). *Servant leadership: A journey into the nature of legitimate Power & greatness.* New York: Paulist Press.
13.   Johnson, C.E. (2005). Meeting the Ethical Challenges of Leadership: Casting light or shadow. Thousand Oaks, CA: Sage.
14.   Kelley, R. (1992). *The power of Followership*.New York: Doubleday/Currency.
15.   Kumuyi, W. (2007). The functions of a servant-leader. New African, 468, pg. 30-31.
16.   McIntosh, G., & Rima, S. (1997). *Overcoming the dark side of leadership: The paradox of personal dysfunction.* Grand Rapid, MI: Baker Books.
17.   Rasmussen, T. (1995). *Creating a Culture of Servant Leadership: A real Life Story*.In Spears, L.C. (1995). *Reflections on Leadership: How Robert K.Greenleaf's Theory of Servant Leadership.* New York: John Wiley & Sons.
18.   Schuster, J. (1994). Transforming your leadership style. *Association Management*, Vol. *46* (1), L39-L43.
19.   Smith, B. N., Montagno, R. V., & Kuzmenko, T. N. (2004). Transformational and servant leadership: Content and contextual comparisons. *Journal of Leadership and Organizational Studies*, 10 (4), 81-91.
20.   Spears, L.C. & Lawrence, M. (2002). *Focus on Leadership: Servant Leadership for the 21^{St} Century.* New York: John Wiley & Sons.
21.   Stone, A.G., Russell, R.F & Patterson, K. (2003). *Transformational Versus Servant Leadership-A difference in Leader Focus.* Paper presented at the servant Leadership Roundtable at Regent University, Virginia Beach, VA, on October, 16, 2003.
22.   Tracey, J., & Hinkin, T. (1998). Transformational leadership or effective managerial practices? *Group & Organization Management*. Volume *23*, 220- 236.
23.   Tucker, B.A. & Russell, R.F. (2004). The Influence of the Transformational Leader. *Journal of Leadership and Organizational Studies*, Vol. 10(4).
24.   Van Eeden, R., Cillers, F., Van Deventer, V. (2008). Leadership styles and associated personality traits: Support for the conceptualization of transactional and transformational leadership. South African Journal of Psychology, 38, p253-267.
25.   Washington, R.R. (2007). *Empirical Relationship among servant, transformational and transactional leadership: Similarities, differences and correlations with job satisfaction and organizational commitment*. PhD Dissertation. Auburn University. ATT 3265529.
26.   Weber, E. & Khademian, A. N (2008). Wicked Problems, Knowledge, challenges, and collaborative Capacity Builders in Network Settings. Public Administrative Review, Vol.68 (2), 334-349.

27. Whetstone, J.T. (2002). Personalism and moral leadership: The servant leader with a transforming. Business Ethics: A European Review, Vol. *11*(4), 385-392.

Chapter 10
Transactional Leadership: Model for Bureaucratic Public Organizations

1. Davidhizer, R., & Shearer, R. (1997). Giving encouragement as a transformational leadership technique. *Health Care Supervisor,* Volume *15,* 16-21.
2. Hodgetts, R.M., Luthans, F. & Doh, J.P. (2005). *International management: Culture, strategy, and behavior*, 6th Ed. New York: The McGraw-Hill Companies.
3. Kanungo, R.N. (2001) Ethical Values of transactional and transformational leaders. *Canadian journal of Administrative Sciences*, Volume 18(4), pp.257-265.
4. King, S. (1994). What is the latest on leadership? *Management Development Review*, Vol. *7,* 7-9.
5. McShane, S.L. & Von Glinov, M. A. (2005). *Organizational behavior*. New York: The McGraw-Hill.
6. Mink, O. (1992). Creating new organizational paradigms for change. International *Journal of Quality & Reliability Management*, Volume *9*, pp.21-23.
7. Trottier, T, Van Wart, M., & Wang, X. (2008). Examining the Nature and Significance of Leadership in Government Organizations. *Public Administration Review*, Vol.*68* (2) pp. 319-334.
8. Tucker, B.A. & Russell, R.F. (2004). The Influence of the Transformational Leader. *Journal of Leadership and Organizational Studies,* Volume 10(4).
9. Washington, R.R. (2007). *Empirical Relationship among servant, transformational and transactional leadership: Similarities, differences and correlations with job satisfaction and organizational commitment*. PhD Dissertation. Auburn University. ATT 3265529.

Chapter 11
Transformational leadership: Model for Public Organizations Undergoing Changes.

1. Aldoory, L., & Toth, E. (2004). Leadership and gender in public relations: Perceived Effectiveness of transformational and transactional leadership styles. *Journal of Public Relations Research*, Vol. *16*(2), 157-183.
2. Ardichvili, A. & Kuchinke, P (2002). Leadership Styles and Cultural Values among Managers and Subordinates: Comparative Study of Four countries of the Former Soviet Union, Germany and the U.S. *Human Resource Development International, 5*(1).
3. Baliga, B.R. & Hunt, J.G. (1988). An organizational life Cycle approach to Leadership.In Hunt, J.G., Baliga, B.R.Dachler, H.P.Schieshei, C.A.*Emerging Leadership Vistas*. Lexington, MA: Lexington Books.
4. Bardwick, J.M. (1996). *Peacetime management and wartime leadership.* In Hessekbein, F; Goldsmith, M; & Beckhard, R.*The leader of the future.* San Francisco, CA: Jossey-Bass.
5. Bass, B. M. (1998). *Transformational leadership: Individual, military, and educational impact*. Enbaum, Mahwah, New Jersey.
6. Bass, B.M. & Avolio, B.J. (1994). *Improving Organizational Effectiveness through Transformational Leadership*. Thousand Oaks, CA: Sage.
7. Benis, W. Nanus, B. (1985). *Leaders: The Strategies for Taking Charge*.New York: Harper & Row.
8. Burns, J.M. (1978). *Leadership*. New York: Harper & Row.
9. Davidhizer, R., & Shearer, R. (1997). Giving encouragement as a transformational leadership technique. *Health Care Supervisor,* Vol. *15,* 16-21.
10. Denhardt, R. B., Denhardt, J.V. & Aristigueta, M.P. (2008). *Managing human behavior in public & nonprofit organizations*. Thousand Oaks, CA: Sage.
11. Herrington, J., Bonem, M., & Furr, J. (2000). *Leading congregational change*. San Francisco: Jossey-Bass.

12. Johnson, C.E. (2005). *Meeting the Ethical challenges of Leadership: casting light or shadow.* Thousand Oaks: Sage Publishers.
13. Kane, T.D. & Tremble, T.R. (2000). Transformational leadership effects at different levels of the army. *Military Psychology, 12*(2), 137-160
14. Mink, O. (1992). Creating new organizational paradigms for change. International *Journal of Quality & Reliability Management*, Volume *9*, pp.21-23.
15. Kelley, E. & Kelloway, E.K. (2012). Context matters testing a model of remote leadership. Journal of leadership & organizational studies, vol.19 (4), 437-449.
16. Seltzer, J. & Bass, B.M. (1990). Transformational leadership: Beyond initiation and consideration. *Journal of Management, 16*(6), 693-70.
17. Smith, B. N., Montagno, R. V., & Kuzmenko, T. N. (2004). Transformational and servant leadership: Content and contextual comparisons. *Journal of Leadership and Organizational Studies,* 10 (4), 81-91.
18. Tichy, N.M. & Devanna, M.A. (1986). *The Transformational Leader.* New York: John Wiley.
19. Tompkins, J.R. 2005 p. 381. Tompkins, J.R. (2005). *Organizational theory and Public Management.* Boston, MA: Thomson-Wadsworth.
20. Trautmann, K.Maher, J.K. & Motley, D.G. (2007). Learning Strategies as Predictors of Transformational Leadership: the case of nonprofit managers. *Leadership & Organization Development Journal.* Bradford, Vol. *28* (3).
21. Tucker, B.A. & Russell, R.F. (2004). The Influence of the Transformational Leader. *Journal of Leadership and Organizational Studies,* Vol. 10(4).
22. Yukl, G. (2006). *Leadership in organizations.* 6th Ed. Upper Saddle River, NJ: Prentice Hall.

Chapter 12
Servant Leadership: Model for Religious Groups, Charitable Organizations, and advocacy Movements

1. Carver, J. (2002). *The Unique double servant-leadership role of the board chair.* In Spears, L.C. & Lawerence, M. (2002). *Focus on leadership: Servant leadership for the 21st century.* (pp.189-209). New York: John Wiley & Sons.
2. Denhardt, R. B., Denhardt, J.V. & Aristigueta, M.P. (2008). *Managing human behavior in public & nonprofit organizations*. Thousand Oaks, CA: Sage.
3. Greenleaf, R. K. (1977). *Servant leadership: A journey into the nature of legitimate Power & greatness.* New York: Paulist Press.
4. Howatson-Jones, I.L. (2004). The servant leader. *Nursing Management. Vol. 11* No. 3. RCN Publishing Company Limited.
5. Johnson, C.E. (2005). Meeting the Ethical Challenges of Leadership: Casting light or shadow. Thousand Oaks, CA: Sage.
6. Laub, J.A. (1999). *Assessing the servant organization. Development of the servant Organizational Leadership Assessment (SOLA) instrument.* Florida Atlantic University Dissertation.
7. Maslow, A. (1970). *Motivation and Personality.*2nd Ed.New York: Harper and Rowe.
8. Smith, B. N., Montagno, R. V., & Kuzmenko, T. N. (2004). Transformational and servant leadership: Content and contextual comparisons. *Journal of Leadership and Organizational Studies,* 10 (4), 81-91.
9. Spears, L.C. (1998) *Insights on leadership: Service, stewardship, spirit and servant Leadership.* New York: John Wiley & Sons.
10. Stone, A.G., Russell, R.F & Patterson, K. (2003). *Transformational Versus Servant Leadership-A difference in Leader Focus.* Paper presented at the servant Leadership Roundtable at Regent University, Virginia Beach, VA, on October, 16, 2003.

11. Washington, R.R. (2007). *Empirical Relationship among servant, transformational and transactional leadership: Similarities, differences and correlations with job satisfaction and organizational commitment.* PhD Dissertation. Auburn University. ATT 3265529.
12. Wong, P.T.P. (2003.*An Opponent-process Model of Servant Leadership and a Typology of Leadership Styles.* Paper presented at the servant Leadership Roundtable at Regent University, Virginia Beach, VA, on October, 16, 2003.

Chapter 13
Sources and Constructs of Power in Public Organizations

1. Denhardt, R. B., Denhardt, J.V. & Aristigueta, M.P. (2008). *Managing human behavior in public & nonprofit organizations.* Thousand Oaks, CA: Sage.
2. McShane, S.L. & Von Glinov, M. A. (2005). *Organizational behavior.* New York: The McGraw-Hill.

Chapter 14
Uses of Power and Authority in Public Organizations

1. Daft, R (1995). Understanding Management. New York: The Dryden Press.
2. Denhardt, R. B., Denhardt, J.V. & Aristigueta, M.P. (2008). *Managing human behavior in public & nonprofit organizations.* Thousand Oaks, CA: Sage.
3. Kreitner, R. & Kinicki, A. (2004). *Organizational behavior.* New York: McGraw-Hill.
4. McShane, S.L. & Von Glinov, M. A. (2005). *Organizational behavior.* New York: The McGraw-Hill.
5. Shafritz, J.M. & Ott, J.S. (2001). Classics of Organizational Theory.New York: Harcourt College Publishers.

Chapter 15
Gaining Power: Structures and Power Plays

1. Denhardt, R. B., Denhardt, J.V. & Aristigueta, M.P. (2008). *Managing human behavior in public & nonprofit organizations.* Thousand Oaks, CA: Sage.
2. Fairholm, Gilbert (1993) *Organizational Power Politics: Tactics in Organizational Leadership,* 2nd Ed. Santa Barbara, Ca: Praeger

Chapter 16
Powerlessness and Power Equalization

1. Denhardt, R. B., Denhardt, J.V. & Aristigueta, M.P. (2008). *Managing human behavior in public & nonprofit organizations.* Thousand Oaks, CA: Sage.

Chapter 17
Nature of Public Organizations and their Leaderships

1. Ahn, M. J; Adamson, J. A. & Dornbusch, D. (2004). From leaders to leadership: Managing change. *The Journal of Leadership and Organizational Studies, 10* (4).
2. Ardichvili, A. & Kuchinke, P (2002). Leadership Styles and Cultural Values among Managers and Subordinates: Comparative Study of Four countries of the Former Soviet Union, Germany and the U.S. *Human Resource Development International, 5*(1).
3. Denhardt, R. B., Denhardt, J.V. & Aristigueta, M.P. (2008). *Managing human behavior in public & nonprofit organizations.* Thousand Oaks, CA: Sage.
4. Den Hartog, D. N., van Muijen, J. J., & Koopman, P. L. (1997). Transactional versus transformational leadership: An analysis of the MLQ. *Journal of Occupational and Organizational Psychology,* Vol. *70,* 19-34.
5. Dooley, K.J. (1997). A complex Adaptive Systems Model of Organizational Change. Nonlinear Dynamics, Psychology, and Life Sciences, Vol. 1 (1).
6. Harrison, G.L.; McKinnon, J.L.Panchapakesan, S& Leung, M. (1994). The influence of Culture on Organizational Design and Planning and Control in Australia and The United States Compared with Singapore and Hong.

185

7. Gomez-Mejia, L.R. & Balkin, D. (2002). *Management*. New York: The McGraw-Hill Companies.
8a. Hosfsede, G. (1983). The cultural Relativity of organizational Practices and Theories, Journal of International business Studies, Vol.14 (2), 75-89.
8b. Hofstede, G. (1985). The Interaction between National and Organizational Value Systems. *Journal of Management Studies*, Vol. 22 (4): 347-357.
9. Kreitner, R. & Kinicki, A. (2004). *Organizational behavior.* New York: McGraw-Hill.
10. McShane, S.L. & Von Glinov, M. A. (2005). *Organizational behavior.* New York: The McGraw-Hill Companies.
11. Masood, S.A., Dani, S.S., Burns, N.D. & Backhouse, C.J. (2005) *Transformational leadership and organizational culture: the situational strength perspective*.
12. Mendonca, M. & Kanungo R.N. (1996). Impact of culture on Performance Management in Developing Countries. *International Journal of Manpower*, vol. 17(4-5), pp.65-76.
13. Shafritz, J. M; Hyde, A. C. & Parkes, S. J. (2004). *Classics of public administration*. 5th Ed. Belmont, CA: Wadsworth/Thompson Learning.
14. Shafritz, J.M., Russell, E.W. & Borick, C.P. (2007). *Introducing Public Administration.* 5th Ed.New York: Pearson-Longman.
15. Stahl, O.G. (1979). Managerial Effectiveness in Developing Countries. *International Review of Administrative Sciences*, Volume *4* (1), pp.1-5.
16. Tompkins, J.R. (2005). *Organizational theory and Public Management*. Boston, MA: Thomson-Wadsworth.
17. Trevion, L.K., Brown, M. & Hartman, L.P. (2003). A qualitative investigation of perceived Executive Ethical Leadership: Perceptions from Inside and Outside the Executive Suite. *Human Relations.* Vol. *56*(1), 5-28.

Chapter 18
The Leader as the 'Master of Change' & Chief Motivator

1. Ackoff, R. (1999). Recreating the Corporation: A design of organizations for the 21st century. New York: Oxford University Press.
2. Ahn, M. J; Adamson, J. A. & Dornbusch, D. (2004). From leaders to leadership: Managing change. *The Journal of Leadership and Organizational Studies*, *10* (4).
3. Burns, J.M. (1978). *Leadership*. New York: Harper & Row.
4. Cohen, M. (1999). Commentary on the Organization Science Special Issue on Complexity. *Organization Science*, Vol. *10*, 373-376.
5. Daft, R (1995). Understanding Management. New York: The Dryden Press.
6. Denhardt, R. B., Denhardt, J.V. & Aristigueta, M.P. (2008). *Managing human behavior in public & nonprofit organizations*. Thousand Oaks, CA: Sage.
7. Giley, A. (2005). *The Manager as Change Leader*.Westport, CT: Praeger.
8. Johnson, C.E. (2005). Meeting the Ethical Challenges of Leadership: Casting light or shadow. Thousand Oaks, CA: Sage.
9. Koteen, J. ((1997). *Strategic Management in Public and Nonprofit Organizations: Managing Public Concerns in an Era of Limits.* Westport; Connecticut: Praeger.
10. Kotter, J.P. (1996). *Leading Change*. Boston: Harvard Business school press.
11. Krishnan, V.R. (2001) Value systems of transformational leaders. *Leadership & Organizational Development Journal*, Vol. *22*(3), 126-131.
12. Mackenzie, M.L. (2007). Leadership in the Information Age: A culture of continual Change. Bulletin of the American society for information science and Technology. Vol. 33(4).
13. Masood, et al. (2006). Masood, S.A., Dani, S.S., Burns, N.D. & Backhouse, C.J. (2005) *Transformational leadership and organizational culture: the situational strength perspective*.

14. Smith, B. N., Montagno, R. V., & Kuzmenko, T. N. (2004). Transformational and servant leadership: Content and contextual comparisons. *Journal of Leadership and Organizational Studies,* 10 (4), 81-91.
15. Trottier, T, Van Wart, M., & Wang, X. (2008). Examining the Nature and Significance of Leadership in Government Organizations. *Public Administration Review*, Volume *68* (2) pp. 319-334.
16. Upshur-Myles, C.C. (2007).What followers want from Leaders: Capitalizing on Diversity. *Nonprofit World.Vol. 25* (5).
17. Weber, E. & Khademian, A. N (2008). Wicked Problems, Knowledge, challenges, and collaborative Capacity Builders in Network Settings. Public Administrative Review, Vol.68 (2), 334-349.
18. Whetstone, J.T. (2002). Personalism and moral leadership: The servant leader with a transforming. Business Ethics: A European Review, Vol. *11*(4), 385-392.

Chapter 19
Leadership Strategies during Organizational Changes

1. Buchanan, .D; Fitzgerald, L; Ketley, D., Gollop, R; Jones, J; Lamont, S. S., Neath, A. &Whitby, E. (2005). No Going Back: A Review of the Literature on Sustaining Organizational Change. International Journal of Management Reviews, Vol. 7 (3). .189-205.
2. Clawson, A. (2006). *Level Three Leadership: Getting Below the Surface*. 3rd Ed.Upper Saddle River, NJ: Pearson/Prentice Hall.
3. Cuthertson, J. (2003) Business across Cultures. *Business Book Review*.Vol.22 (19).
4. Denhardt, R. B., Denhardt, J.V. & Aristigueta, M.P. (2008). *Managing human behavior in public & nonprofit organizations*. Thousand Oaks, CA: Sage.
5. Dym, B (1999). Resistance in Organizations: How to Recognize, Understand, &Respond to It. *Journal of the Organizational Development Network, Vol.31* (1).
6. Fahey, L. & Narayanan, V. K. (1986). Macro environmental analysis for strategic Management. St Paul, MN: West.
7. Felfe, J. & Schyns, B. (2004). Is similarity in Leadership related to organizational Outcomes? The case of transformational Leadership. Journal of Leadership & Organizational studies, Volume 10(4).
8. Gilley, A., McMillian, H. S., & Gilley, J. W., (2009). Organizational change and characteristics of leadership effectiveness. *Journal of Leadership and Organizational studies*, *16* (1).
9. Gordon, G.L. (2005). Strategic planning for local government. Washington, DC: International City/County Management Association.
9a. Heilpern, J. D., & Nadler, D. A. (1992). *Implementing Total Quality Management: A process of cultural Change*. In D. A. Nadler, M. S. Gerstein & R. B. Shaw (Eds.), *Organizational architecture. Designs for Changing organizations.* San Francisco, CA: Jossey-Bass.
10. Howard, A. (1997). High Involvement Leadership: Moving from talk to action. Empowerment in Organizations, MCB University Press, June 1997.
11. Kotter, J.P. (2012). Leading Change. Boston, MA: Harvard Business Review Press.
12. Koteen, J. (1997). *Strategic Management in Public and Nonprofit Organizations: Managing Public Concerns in an Era of Limits.* Westport; Connecticut: Praeger.
13. Kreitner, R. & Kinicki, A. (2004). *Organizational behavior.* New York: McGraw-Hill.
14. Mackenzie, M.L. (2007). Leadership in the Information Age: A culture of

Continual Change. *Bulletin of the American society for information Science and Technology.* Vol. 33(4).

15. McShane, S.L. & Von Glinov, M. A. (2005). *Organizational behavior.* New York: The McGraw-Hill.
16. Mendonca, M. & Kanungo R.N. (1996). Impact of culture on Performance Management in Developing Countries. *International Journal of Manpower*, volume 17(4-5), pp.65-76.
17. Shafritz, J.M., Russell, E.W. & Borick, C.P. (2007). *Introducing Public Administration.*5thEd.New York: Pearson-Longman.
18. .Simmons, A. (2001). *The Story Factor: Inspiration, Influence, and Persuasion Through the Art of Storytelling.* New York: Basic Books.
19. .Stacey, R.D., Griffin, D. & Shaw, P. (2002).Complexity and Management: Fad or Radical Challenge to Systems Thinking. London: Rutledge.
20 Trautmann, K.Maher, J.K. & Motley, D.G. (2007). Learning Strategies as Predictors of Transformational Leadership: the case of nonprofit managers. *Leadership & Organization Development Journal*. Bradford, Vol. *28* (3).
21. Yazeen, Z. & Okour, A. (2012). Managing organizational change: Decision's maker perceptions in the UAE manufacturing industry. *International Journal of Research Studies in Management*, Vol. 1 (1), 97-108.

Chapter 20
Strategies for Optimizing Leadership

1. Avolio, B.J.Luthans, F. & Walumbwa, F.O. (2004). Authentic Leadership: Theory- Building for Veritable Sustained Performance. In Kim C. (2009) Developing Effective Leadership Skills. Book review. *Public Administration Review.* May/June 2009.
1a. Bajer, J. (2009). Today, either everyone is a leader, or nobody is. *Strategic HR Review*, 8(5), 38- 39.
2. Berman, E.M., West, J.P. & Bonczek, S.J. (2004). *The Ethics Edge. International City/County Management Association.* Washington D.C.
3. Burack, E.H., Burack, M.D., Miller, D.M. & Morgan, K. (1994). *New Paradigm Approaches in Strategic Human Resource Mangement.*Group and Organization Management.Vol.19.141-159.
4. Cascio, W.F. (1995). *Managing Human Resources: Productivity, Quality of Work Life, Profits.* New York: McGraw-Hill.
5. Denhardt, R. B., Denhardt, J.V. & Aristigueta, M.P. (2008). *Managing human behavior in public & nonprofit organizations*. Thousand Oaks, CA: Sage.
6. DiGiammarino, F. In Kim, C. (2009). Developing Effective Leadership Skills. Book review. *Public Administration Review*. May/June 2009.
7. Hellriegel, D. & Slocum, J.W. (2007). *Organizational Behavior.*Mason, OH: Thomson/South-Western.
8. Hodgetts, R.M., Luthans, F. & Doh, J.P. (2005). *International management: Culture, strategy, and behavior*, 6th Ed. New York: The McGraw-Hill Companies.
9. Howard, A. (1997). High Involvement Leadership: Moving from talk to action. *Empowerment in Organizations*, MCB University Press.
10. Kim, C. (2009). Developing Effective Leadership Skills. Book review. *Public Administration Review*. May/June 2009.
11. Kotter, J. (1990). *A force for Change. How Leadership Differs From Management.* New York: Guilford Press.
12. Kreitner, R. & Kinicki, A. (2004). *Organizational behavior.* New York: McGraw-Hill.
13. Larson, C.E. & LaFasto, F.M. (1989).*Teamwork.* Newbury Park, CA: Sage Publications.

14. Lynham, S.A. & Chermack, T.J. (2006). Responsible Leadership For Performance: A Theoretical Model and hypothesis. *Journal of Leadership & Organizational Studies, Vol. 12*(4).
15. Meynell, F. (2005). A second-order approach to evaluating and facilitating organizational Change. *Action Research,* Volume *3*(2), 211-231.
16. McShane, S.L. & Von Glinov, M. A. (2005). *Organizational behavior.* New York: The McGraw-Hill.
17. Peters, T. & Waterman, R.H. (1982). *In Search of Excellence: Lessons from America's Best-Run Companies.* London: Harper and Row.
18. Pfeffer, J. (1994). *Competitive Advantage through People.* Boston Mass: Harvard Business Press.
19. Stroh, L.K., & Caligiuri, P.M. (1998). Strategic Human Resources: A new Source for Competitive Advantage in The Global Arena. *The international Journal of Human Resource Mangement,* 9(1).
20. Trautmann, K.Maher, J.K. & Motley, D.G. (2007). Learning Strategies as Predictors of Transformational Leadership: the case of nonprofit managers. *Leadership & Organization Development Journal.* Bradford, Vol. *28* (3).
21. Trevion, L.K., Brown, M. & Hartman, L.P. (2003). A qualitative investigation of perceived Executive Ethical Leadership: Perceptions from Inside and Outside the Executive Suite. *Human Relations.* Vol. 56(1), .5-28.
22. Watkins. & Cooperrider, D. (2000). Appreciative Inquiry: A Transformative Paradigm. *Journal of the Organizational Development Network, Vol. 32* (1).

<h2 style="text-align:center">Chapter 21</h2>
<h3 style="text-align:center">Frameworks for strategic Decision Making</h3>

1. Denhardt, R. B., Denhardt, J.V. & Aristigueta, M.P. (2008). *Managing human behavior in public & nonprofit organizations.* Thousand Oaks, CA: Sage.
2. Kingdon, J.W. (2003). Agendas, Alternatives and Public Policies. New York: Addison-Wesley Educational Publishers, Inc.
3. Selznick, P. In Shafritz, J.M. & Ott, J.S. (2001). *Classics of Organizational Theory.* .New York: Harcourt College Publishers.

<h2 style="text-align:center">Chapter 22</h2>
<h3 style="text-align:center">Techniques for Decision Making</h3>

1. Denhardt, R. B., Denhardt, J.V. & Aristigueta, M.P. (2008). *Managing human behavior in public & nonprofit organizations.* Thousand Oaks, CA: Sage.

<h2 style="text-align:center">Chapter 23</h2>
<h3 style="text-align:center">Strategic Planning for Optimizing Leadership</h3>

1. Anderson, J.E. (2006). Public PolicyMaking. 6th Ed.New York: Houghton Mifflin Company.
2. Daft, R (1995). Understanding Management. New York: The Dryden Press.
3. Daley, D. M. (1992). Performance Appraisal in the public sector: Techniques and applications.
   Westport, CT: Quorum Books.
4. Digman, L.A. (1999) Strategic management: concepts, processes and decisions .Houston, TX: Dame Publication.
5. Gordon, G.L. (2005). Strategic planning for local government. Washington, DC: International City/County Management Association.
6. Kingdon, J.W. (2003). Agendas, Alternatives and Public Policies. New York: Addison-Wesley Educational Publishers, Inc.
7. Koteen, J. ((1997). *Strategic Management in Public and Nonprofit Organizations: Managing Public Concerns in an Era of Limits.* Westport; Connecticut: Praeger.

8. Nutt, P.C. & Backoff, R.W. (1992). Strategic management of public and third sector organizations: A handbook for leaders. San Francisco, CA: Jossey-Bass.
9. Shafritz, J. M; Hyde, A. C. & Parkes, S. J. (2004). *Classics of public administration.* 5th Ed. Belmont, CA: Wadsworth/Thompson Learning.
10. Shafritz, J.M., Russell, E.W. & Borick, C.P. (2007). *Introducing Public Administration.*5[th]Ed.New York: Pearson-Longman.
11. Shim, J. K; Siegel, J. G. & Shim, A.I. (2012). Budgeting Basics and Beyond. Hoboken, New Jersey: John Wiley & Sons, Inc.

Chapter 24
Ethics and Values in Public Organizations

1. Anderson, J.E. (2006). Public Policy Making. 6th Ed.New York: Houghton Mifflin Company.
2. Asad, T. (2003). Boundaries and Rights in Islamic Law: *Introduction. Social Research,* 70(3), 683-686.
3. Berman, E.M., Bowman, J.S; West, J.P. & Van Wart, M. (2001). *Human Resource Management in Public Service: Paradoxes, Processes, and Problems.* Sage Publications: Thousand Oaks: CA.
4. Ciulla, J. B. (2004). Leadership Ethics: Mapping the Territory. In J. B. Ciulla, Ethics, the Heart of Leadership 2nd Ed. (pp. 1-24). Westport: Praeger Publishers.
5. Hofstede, G. (1980). Culture's Consequences. : International Differences in Work-Related Values. Beverly Hills, CA: Sage Publications.
6. Hosfsede, G. (1983). The cultural Relativity of organizational Practices and Theories, Journal of International business Studies, Vol.14 (2), pp75-89.
7. Johnson, C.E. (2005). Meeting the Ethical Challenges of Leadership: Casting light or shadow. Thousand Oaks, CA: Sage Publications.
8. Knapp, S. & VandeCreek, L. (2007). When values of different cultures conflict: Ethical decision making in a multicultural context. *Professional Psychology: Research and Practice, 38(6),* 660-666.
9. Mtango, S. (2004). A State of Oppression? *Women Rights in Saudi Arabia. Asia-Pacific on Human Rights and the Law, Vol.*1, 49-67.
19. Patton, C. V. & Sawicki, D. S. (1993). Basic methods of policy analysis and planning. (2nd Ed.). New Jersey: Prentice-Hall.
20. Shafritz, J. M; Hyde, A. C. & Parkes, S. J. (2004). *Classics of public administration.* 5th Ed. Belmont, CA: Wadsworth/Thompson Learning.
21. Swaidan, Z., and Hayes, L.A. 2005. Hofstede theory and cross cultural ethics: conceptualization, review, and research agenda. The Journal of American Academy of Business, Number 2. p. 10-15. Cambridge MA.
22. West, J.P. & Berman, E.M. (Eds.). (2006). *The ethics edge.* (2nd Ed.). Washington, DC: ICMA Press.
23. Wood, A. (2007). Cross-cultural moral philosophy: reflections on Thaddeus Metz: "Toward an African moral theory." *South African Journal of Philosophy.* 26, 4: 336-346.

Chapter 25
General Ethical Perspectives for Public Organizations

1. Airaksinen, T. (2012). The philosophy of professional ethics. In Institutional Issues Involving ethics and justice, Ed. By Robert C. Elliot, vol. 1, in Encyclopedia of Life support systems (EOLSS), under the auspices of UNESCO, EOLSS Publisher, Paris, France.
2. Cavalier, R. (2005). The impact of the Internet on our moral lives. Albany, NY: State University of New York Press.
3. Collste, G. (2012). Applied and professional ethics. Kemanusiaan, vol. 19 (1), 17-33.
4. Johnson, C.E. (2005). *Meeting the Ethical Challenges of Leadership: Casting light or shadow.* Thousand Oaks, CA: Sage.

5. Lan, Z. & Anders, K.K. (2000). A Paradigmatic View of Contemporary Public Administration Research: An Empirical Test. Administration & Society, Vol. 32(2), pp138-165.
6. Swaidan, Z; Vitell, S.J; Rawwas, Y.A. (August, 2003). Consumer Ethics: Determinants of Ethical Beliefs of African Americans. Journal of Business Ethics.46, 2, 177.
7. The Guardian (2011). Shell accepts liability for two oil spills in Nigeria. The Guardian, August 3, 2011. http://www.guardian.co.uk/environment/2011/aug/03/shell-liability-oil-spills-Nigeria.
8. The Shell BP (2016). Deepwater Horizon accident and response. http://www.bp.com/en_us/bp-us/commitment-to-the-gulf-of-mexico/deepwater-horizon-accident.html
9. UNEP (2011). Environmental assessment of Ogoniland. http://www.unep.org/disastersandconflicts/CountryOperations/Nigeria/EnvironmentalAssessmentofOgonilandreport/tabid/54419/

Chapter: 26
Applications of Values and Ethics in Public Organizations

1. Berman, E.M., Bowman, J.S; West, J.P. & Van Wart, M. (2001). *Human Resource Management in Public Service: Paradoxes, Processes, and Problems.* Sage Publications, Inc: Thousand Oaks: CA.
2. Cooper, T.L. & Bryer, T.A. (2007). William Robertson: Exemplar of Politics and Public Management Rightly Understood. *Public Administration Review.*Volume *67* (5), p.816.
3. Digman, L.A. (1999) Strategic management: concepts, processes and decisions. Houston, TX: Dame Publication.
4. Hill, R.B. (1996). *History of Work Ethic.* Retrieved June 16, 2008 from http://www.coe.uga.edu/workethic/hatmp.htm.
5. Fisher, C.D., Schoenfeldt, L.F. & Shaw. B. (1993). *Human Resource Management.* 2nd Ed.MA; Boston: Houghton Mifflin Company.
6. Maywood, A. G. (1982). Vocational education and the work ethic. *Canadian Vocational Journal, 18*(3), 7-12.
7. Rodgers, D. T. (1978). *The work ethic in industrial America, 1850-1920.* Chicago: The University of Chicago Press.
8. Rose, M. (1985). *Reworking the work ethic: Economic values and socio-cultural politics.* London: Schocken.
9. Shafritz, J. M; Hyde, A. C. & Parkes, S. J. (2004). *Classics of public administration.* 5th Ed. Belmont, CA: Wadsworth/Thompson Learning.
10. Shafritz, J.M., Russell, E.W. & Borick, C.P. (2007). *Introducing Public Administration.*5thEd.New York: Pearson-Longman.
11. Tilgher, A. (1930). *Homo faber: Work through the ages.* Translated by D. C. Fisher. New York: Harcourt Brace.
12. Thompson, D. F. (1985). The possibility of Administrative ethics. *Public Administrative Review, 45* (5), 555-561.

Chapter 27
Corruption: Ethical Deviance in Public Organizations

1. Davis, J.H. & Ruhe, J.A. (2003) Perception of country corruption: antecedents and outcomes. *Journal of Business Ethics,* Vol. 43(4), .275.
2. Geo-JaJa, M. A. & Mangum, G. L. (2000). The Foreign Corrupt Practices Act's Consequences for U.S. Trade: The Nigerian Example. *Journal of Business Ethics,* Vol. 24 (3). Part 1, 245-256.

3. Haines, D.W. (2003-4). Fatal choices: The routinization of deceit, incompetence, and corruption. In West, J.P. & Berman, E.M. (Eds.). (2006). The ethics edge. (2nd Ed.). Washington, DC: ICMA Press.
4. Johnson, C.E. (2005). Meeting the Ethical Challenges of Leadership: Casting light or shadow. Thousand Oaks, CA: Sage Publications.
5. Lo, S.S.H. (2006). Ethical Governance and Anti-Corruption in Greater China: A Comparison of Mainland China, Hong Kong and Macao. CPSA/ACSP papers. Htt://:www.cpsa-acsp.ca/papers-2006/Lo.pdf.
6. Trautman, N. (2000, June). The corruption continuum: How law enforcement organizations become corrupt. In West, J.P. & Berman, E.M. (Eds.). (2006). The ethics edge. (2nd Ed.). Washington, DC: ICMA Press.

Chapter 28
Ethical Leadership in Public Organizations

1. Berman, E.M., West, J.P. & Bonczek, S.J. (2004). *The Ethics Edge. International City/County Management Association.* Washington D.C.
2. Clapp-Smith, R., Vogelgesang, G.R; & Avey, J.B. (2009). Authentic Leadership and Positive Psychological Capital: The Mediating role of trust at Group level of Analysis. *Journal of Leadership & Organizational Studies,* Vol. *15*(3), pp.227-240.
3. Denhardt, R. B., Denhardt, J.V. & Aristigueta, M.P. (2008). *Managing human behavior in public & nonprofit organizations.* Thousand Oaks, CA: Sage.
4. Gardner, W.L., Avolio, B.J; Luthans, F.May, D.R. & Walumbwa, F. (2005). Can you see the real me? A self-based model of authentic, Leader and Follower development. *Leadership Quarterly,* Vol. *16,* 343-372.
5. Johnson, C.E. (2005). Meeting the Ethical Challenges of Leadership: Casting light or shadow. Thousand Oaks, CA: Sage.
6. Lan, Z. & Anders, K.K. (2000). A Paradigmatic View of Contemporary Public Administration Research: An Empirical Test. Administration & Society, Vol. 32(2), pp138-165.
7. Nye Jr., J. (2008, March 28). Transformational leaders are not always better. *Christian Science Monitor,* 100(86), 9-9.
8. Trevion, L.K., Brown, M. & Hartman, L.P. (2003). A qualitative investigation of perceived Executive Ethical Leadership: Perceptions from Inside and Outside the Executive Suite. *Human Relations.* Vol. *56*(1), pp.5-28.
9. West, J.P. & Berman, E.M. (Eds.). (2006). The ethics edge. (2nd Ed.). Washington, DC: ICMA Press.

www.ingramcontent.com/pod-product-compliance
Lightning Source LLC
Chambersburg PA
CBHW060553200326
41521CB00007B/560